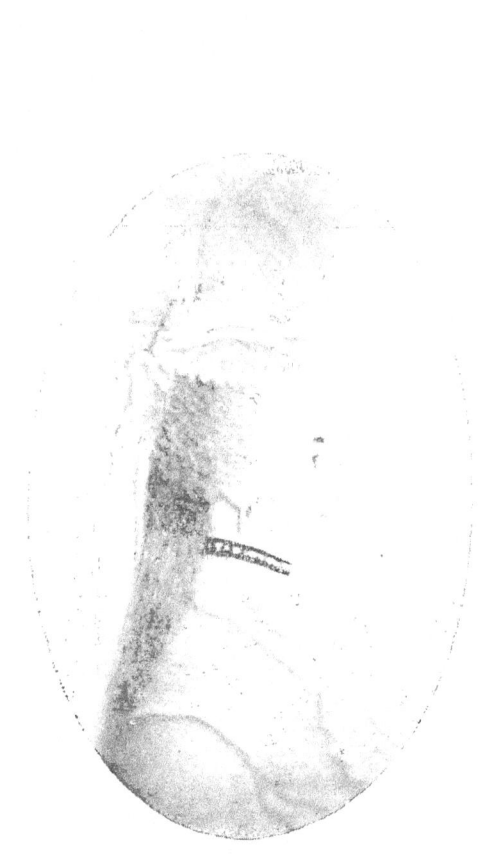

GRACIA DURA BIN
THE GRECIAN WIFE OF DR. TURNBULL

Dr. Andrew Turnbull

and
The New Smyrna Colony
of
Florida

Carita Doggett, A.B., A.M.

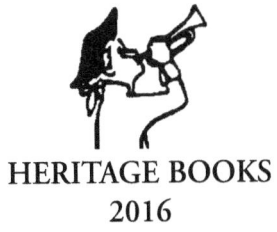

HERITAGE BOOKS
2016

HERITAGE BOOKS
AN IMPRINT OF HERITAGE BOOKS, INC.

Books, CDs, and more—Worldwide

For our listing of thousands of titles see our website
at
www.HeritageBooks.com

A Facsimile Reprint
Published 2016 by
HERITAGE BOOKS, INC.
Publishing Division
5810 Ruatan Street
Berwyn Heights, Md. 20740

Entered according to Act of Congress, in the year 1919 by
Carita Doggett,
in the office of the Librarian of Congress at Washington.

Originally published: Florida
The Drew Press
1919

— Publisher's Notice —
In reprints such as this, it is often not possible to remove blemishes from the original. We feel the contents of this book warrant its reissue despite these blemishes and hope you will agree and read it with pleasure.

International Standard Book Numbers
Paperbound: 978-0-7884-0019-3
Clothbound: 978-0-7884-6459-1

To
MY FATHER,

Whose interest and encouragement
made the work of this book
a pleasure for me.

CONTENTS

I—The Outlaw Province.................. 11
II—The Making of New Smyrna.......... 29
III—The Uprising of 1768.................. 49
IV—England Lends Financial Aid......... 63
V—Governor Grant Leaves Florida........ 75
VI—The New Governor.................... 85
VII—Spanish Intrigue...................... 95
VIII—Turnbull and Drayton vs. Tonyn and Moultrie........................... 109
IX—The Flight to England............... 129
X—The Fall of New Smyrna.............. 157
XI—The Fight for the Property.......... 179
Bibliography 197
Index 213

ILLUSTRATIONS

GRACIA DURA BIN, WIFE OF DR. TURNBULL
(Frontispiece)

THE GRACEFUL VARIETY OF FOLIAGE............	25
ONE OF THE MANY COQUINA-LINED WELLS.......	49
FOUNDATIONS OF THE FORT.....................	62
GLIMPSE OF ONE OF THE TURNBULL CANALS......	93
RUINS OF THE OLD MISSION....................	189

PREFACE

Every old inhabitant of Florida knows of Andrew Turnbull. Most tourists on the East Coast have read Susan Turnbull, that romantic and imaginary version of his Minorcan colony, by Archibald Clavering Gunter, and have taken pictures of the old Sugar Mill and "Turnbull's Castle" at New Smyrna. If an old resident is asked about him, he says "Turnbull was a bad sort,"—in fact Gunter makes a kind of wicked ogre out of him; so that about the great coquina ruins, cleft with palm trees, hovers a sinister mist of traditions.

Reminders of Turnbull are plentiful throughout the State. On the palm covered banks of the North Indian River stands New Smyrna itself, named for Smyrna, Asia Minor, the birthplace of Turnbull's wife. The pretty modern town is threaded with the main canals of the old colony and water still runs through them in a musical monotone, from Turnbull's great hammock lands to the river. Every year a large winter colony returns to picturesque homes and groves, and the new colonists spend many pleasant hours speculating over the works of their predecessors—the sunken pier, the lovely arches of the old Mission, many stone wells and the heavy foundations of the fort. Then the Turnbull family has continued to be prominent in Florida, and the dark-eyed descendants of those Minorcans who came with him to New Smyrna, a hundred and fifty years ago, now live in St. Augustine and hand down among themselves lurid traditions of the old colony. Nothing dependable from a historical standpoint has ever been attempted in regard to this, the largest colony which ever came to America in a body, but the strange chance of literary fortune preserved and gave prominence to the most garbled account of Turnbull's management there. Despite the fact that his contemporaries, Governor Grant, Chief Justice Drayton, Schoepf, a German traveler, and Mease, a learned Frenchman, testified to his earnest devotion to his colonists, yet it remained for Bernard Romans, a civil engineer with a literary turn, to recall the frightful tales of his Minorcan draughtsman, and to write, for all subsequent historians, the story of Andrew Turnbull. Even his worst enemies did not in his day believe such stories as Romans set forth in his eloquent style. They made extravagant charges against him for political reasons, which were disproved by Turnbull in court, but Romans wrote, years after the events themselves, an account based on what his employee remembered. But he made a good story and Floridians became satisfied that they had harbored a second King Leopold at New Smyrna.

In the meantime, the real account had moved to London and settled in that treasure-house of romantic fact, the British Colonial Office. There it remained secure, like a reasonable man, biding his time, against a day when people would be ready and willing to hear the whole story. And it is so startlingly different from the present idea of Turnbull and his colonists that, it seems to me, both sides, if there remain sides on this question, may be interested to learn of it for themselves. As is often the case in collecting the facts of a dispute, the source of the trouble was a far cry from Turnbull and his colonists; and the trouble itself insignificant, when considered in its proper place in the course of most interesting events.

Only documentary evidence has been relied upon, no statements from secondary sources of information have been accepted without careful verification, and copies of all the original manuscripts have been collected and filed with the Florida Historical Society. These manuscripts are the only copies in this country. A list of these papers has also been appended to this volume, and it will be evident at a glance how full and consecutive this information is. The phraseology and spelling from them have been faithfully copied, wherever quoted, and except for a very few obsolete words and one or two grammatical constructions, it will be readily seen that their authors might well rank as masters of modern English prose.

ABBREVIATIONS IN MONOGRAPHIC REFERENCES

Public Record Office documents in London.

C. O.—Colonial Office.
(e. g. 5/544=Class 5, Volume 544).
P. C.—Privy Council.
W. O.—War Office.
T.—Treasury.
A. O.—Audit Office.

CHAPTER I

THE OUTLAW PROVINCE

FLORIDA, in the first half of the eighteenth century, was a thorn in the side of the British colonies, for Spain carried on flanking attacks against their commerce and farming from this outlaw stronghold. Carolina planters often lost their slaves across its boundaries and the Spanish governor at St. Augustine refused to antagonize his Indian allies by commanding their return; so many an English slave-hunting expedition, aggravated the quarrel by invading his territory in a search for their property. Pirates of the long, lonely coast line preyed on the tobacco exports and the sorely needed supply ships of England and her colonies, and finally the new Georgia settlement, under Oglethorpe, raised a dispute in 1736, over the Florida boundary line, which brought on twenty-nine years of open warfare between England and Spain.

There followed the ridiculously weak attempts of Georgia to punish Florida, and retaliatory expeditions, by the Spaniards: Oglethorpe camped on Anastasia Island, opposite St. Augustine, and shelled the compact little fortress until his provisions gave out, and a Spanish fleet sailed into St. Simon's and drove the inhabitants inland. But nothing was decided by these excursions. In 1762, however, an astonishing coup by England started the international gamesters to trading. Havana, the pride and center of Spanish America, fell before a British force, and with this rich prize in her hands, England was ready to bargain for peace. This was arranged by the Peace of Paris in 1763, when Spain gave East and West Florida to England in exchange for Havana. At the same time, France yielded Canada to

England, thus bringing to the highwater mark English power in the New World.

At first sight, East and West Florida seem to us to have been an enormous price to pay for Cuba. East Florida was what we now know as Florida, minus the small section west of the Apalachicola River, while West Florida included the coast of Alabama, Mississippi and a part of Louisiana. This enormous region was practically undeveloped, however, in spite of one hundred and ninety years of Spanish rule. Three small towns (St. Augustine, Pensacola and Mobile) were the only attempts the Spanish had made at colonizing, and the seven thousand people who were divided among these tiny settlements were of the civil and military class and had received no encouragement from Spain in agricultural ventures, therefore trade with the Indians was their only business.

These Indians of Florida were a special problem in themselves, little understood by

DR. ANDREW TURNBULL

the settlers. It must be remembered that they were the bewildering fragments of many races; exiles from Georgia tribes, old nations broken in power by Spanish invasions and wanderers seeking fresh hunting grounds, so that there was no league which had authority among them all, and, therefore, no means of reaching an agreement with them, such as Oglethorpe had made with the Creeks. The English governors were always at a loss to understand why, in spite of treaties and presents to many great chiefs, their settlements were continually plundered and cattle driven off by other Indians.

In spite of these difficulties, England was encouraged to complete her coast possessions by the acquisition of Florida, feeling as she did that she had now proven herself the supreme genius among European powers in colonizing enterprises. From New England to Georgia, prosperous agricultural communities showed the farmer a conqueror, while the French traders and Spanish soldiers were still lost in the immensity of their discoveries. Accordingly, her plan of real estate development was started for Florida in 1763, and books by Bartram, Romans and other writers were the ancestors of that long line of literary praise of Florida which then, just as it does today, dealt less with the actual than with the fancied Florida. In those days, authors were given carte blanche to expatiate on the riches, beauties and luxuries of Florida life, as well as its mild climate, fine soil and valuable products. Parliament added a more substantial persuasion for settlement in 1764, when five hundred pounds a year was set aside as a bounty for the raising of silk, cotton and indigo in East Florida, and extensive land grants were ffered for development. For three years that ounty accumulated and Florida's praises coninued to be sung without moving the British public to respond.

But there was in London at this time a gentleman of some wealth, who had lived in Asia Minor and other Mediterranean countries, where the climate was similar to Florida's.

DR. ANDREW TURNBULL

This man was Dr. Andrew Turnbull, a Scotchman, whose acquaintance in London included the most influential and wealthy men. He convinced a number of them that a settlement in Florida by people accustomed to a warm climate, and the growing of crops suited to that region, would not only be a good investment, but an enterprise encouraged by the government. Turnbull said he was sure of getting a large number of Greeks from Asia Minor to start a colony, for he had lived there for some years and knew that these people were very restive under the galling yoke of Turkey. He was not only thoroughly acquainted with the Greeks of this region, but about seven years previously he had married the daughter of a Greek merchant of Smyrna, Asia Minor, and he felt confident that he would be favorably received as a leader of such a colony to the new province of Florida. Though at that time a prosperous physician in London, forty-eight years old, he was willing to undertake this tremendous pioneer venture, and to bring his wife and family to Florida. His wife, Maria Gracia, was a no less dauntless spirit than he, and played a courageous part in this undertaking. The little miniature of Mrs. Turnbull shows her dressed in the height of Smyrnian fashion, with a small waist and high coiffure and a carriage erect to the point of hauteur, while the set to her lips shows her a lady of much determination and spirit, a true partner for a pioneer doctor. She faced the dangers of the savage new land resolutely, several times ran the affairs of the settlement when business took her husband to New York or London, and raised her seven children to take a creditable part in the history of Florida and South Carolina. Hers was indeed a life of more variety than was granted to most people of her day—to be reared in Asia Minor, to enjoy the life of London society as a young married woman, to establish her family in a wild land, beset by Indians, and to end her days in Charleston, the most aristocratic city of Colonial times, as a leader there by reason of her

DR. ANDREW TURNBULL

cosmopolitan charm and her husband's high position. At the time of the removal to Florida, she was thirty-three years old, at the height of her social career, so that it was a real sacrifice for her to bury herself in the wilderness, and in Turnbull's letters to the Earl of Shelburne, he said that he and his wife often thought with regret of the friends they had left at Bowood and at Shelburne House.[1]

On April 2, 1767, the first partnership agreement concerning the colony was signed by Andrew Turnbull, Sir William Duncan and Sir Richard Temple, Commr. of the Navy.[2] Three adjoining grants of 20,000 acres each had been obtained, one for Duncan, one for Turnbull, one for Temple, the last as trustee in this affair for George Grenville and his heirs. This George Grenville was Prime Minister of England at the time, and felt that he should not act per-

---

(1) Lib. of Congress, British Transcripts, Box 41, Lansdowne Mss. 1219, fo. 34.

(2) Treasury 77/7, Indenture of Mar. 9, 1781.

THE NEW SMYRNA COLONY OF FLORIDA

sonally in the undertaking. The grants were to be operated for a period of seven years at a joint expense not exceeding 9000 pounds and any subsequent grants to the partners were to be treated in the same way. At the end of this period, equal division was to be made between the partners, a committee of seven disinterested persons determining the division, two chosen by each partner and one by the other six members of the committee. A description of the three equal lots should then be drawn from a box by the partners in turn.[1] This was the original outline of the New Smyrna partnership plan which was destined to be changed twice thereafter.

The first land grant issued to Turnbull on June 18, 1766, allowed him to select his tract of 20,000 acres of unclaimed land in East Florida, and therefore it devolved upon him to go to Florida and look over the country. He arrived there with his family in November,

---

(1) Treasury 77/7, First Indenture.

DR. ANDREW TURNBULL

1767,[2] a month which a native knows is usually mild and clear, after the Equinoctial storms. He had to land at St. Augustine, the capital, and the only city on the East coast, and of course paid his respects at once to Governor Grant, who had already been there three years trying to clean up after the Spaniards. James Grant was a soldier who had played a prominent part in the capture of Havana, and his appointment as Governor of Florida was a direct acknowledgment of his services. St. Augustine had been partially burned and destroyed by the departing Spaniards, even the Spanish governor dismantling his beautiful garden in an outburst of hatred against the temporary English commander, a man of arbitrary methods, who had aroused the bitterest opposition. Grant, however, was as fine an administrator as he was a soldier, and his little capital had grown to three thousand inhabitants by this time.

---

(2) C.O. 5/541, pp 199-201, Grant to Shelburne.

THE NEW SMYRNA COLONY OF FLORIDA

Turnbull decided to establish his family here until the new colony was well started,[1] so he took one of the typical Spanish houses of the town, with balconies overhanging the narrow streets and a lovely garden behind high stone walls. Turnbull of course noted with pleasure the great variety of fruits and flowers which grew in his inner court. From the piazza, shaded by Tuscan pillars, he could see first the grape arbor before the entrance, and beyond, his garden, as well as many others, contained fig, guava, plantain, pomegranate, lemon, lime, citron, shaddock, bergamot, China and Seville orange trees. The real beauty of Florida is a cultivated beauty which comes out today in the rare court of the Ponce de Leon Hotel at St. Augustine and the gardens at Palm Beach. Wild Florida landscape is unkempt and weird, and Turnbull was glad to see how much could be done with intelligent care. He also enjoyed the climate, which was so temperate that, according to Moorish cus-

---

(1) C.O. 5/541, pp 199-201.

DR. ANDREW TURNBULL

tom, the houses had been built without fireplaces. There were no windows on the north walls, and when a northeaster blew keen across Matanzas Inlet, a negro brought an urn of glowing coals and set it in his room.

Governor Grant was noted for his hospitality and a brilliant company often gathered at his table to discuss and to settle peaceably the affairs of the province.[1] Though an autocrat who brooked little opposition to his policies, he was genial, and he took an immediate fancy to Dr. Turnbull, of whom it was said that wherever he went, he carried an atmosphere of gaiety and good humor.[2] And so Turnbull always found him a wise and liberal assistant throughout the troubles of the colony's first few years. This was the more remarkable because Grant was accounted stingy about government moneys,[3] and be-

---

(1) Forbes, p. 19.

(2) Charleston Gazette, Mar. 14, 1792.

(3) C.O. 5/555, pp 277-281.

cause Turnbull favored a more democratic policy of government within the province than Grant allowed.

Many prominent men from England and the colonies had moved to St. Augustine, among them, William Drayton, Chief Justice, and Major Moultrie, afterwards Lieutenant Governor of Florida. The former was to become Turnbull's lifelong friend, and the latter an unrelenting enemy. Other Englishmen who had come to Florida, like himself, to build up the new province, were Dennis Rolle, who had started a unique settlement on the St. Johns River, and Mr. Oswald, the owner of a large sugar plantation on the Halifax river; Sir Charles Burdett, Rev. John Forbes, the admiralty judge; Wm. Stark, the historian; Bernard Romans, civil engineer; William Bartram, naturalist, and Rev. Mr. Frazier. As Turnbull's settlement was by far the most ambitious thing ever attempted in Florida, he must have been the center of attention. Grant saw in him a powerful aid for his governing

DR. ANDREW TURNBULL

council, and Turnbull received his appointment to it two months after his return to England.[1] On May 1, 1767, having been appointed Secretary and Clerk of the Council, he felt obliged to resign the office of Clerk of the Crown and Clerk of Common Pleas to which he had been appointed in September,[2] while Grant reported to Lord Hillsborough that, in accordance with the King's command,[3] every effort would be made to assist Dr. Turnbull. William Gerard de Brahm, the government surveyor, was at once consulted as to the best lands available in East Florida and, with the advice of the other planters, Turnbull decided to visit Mosquito Inlet, the first large harbor south of St. Augustine and distant about seventy-five miles. This region was reported to include some of the most valuable lands in the province, and the year he arrived a colony

---

(1) C/O 5/545 p. 25.

(2) Landsdowne Mss. Vol. 88, f.139.

(3) C.O. 5/549 p. 262.

Sande Studio, New Smyrna, Fla.

THE GRACEFUL VARIETY OF FOLIAGE ON THE OLD KING'S ROAD, NEW S

of ship builders had attempted a settlement there on account of the splendid trees in the vicinity.[1]

He sailed down the coast, past what is now known as Ormond and Daytona Beaches, and entered Mosquito Inlet the morning of the second day. The deep blue waters, set in snowy sand-bars, admitted his ship to the North Indian River, passing by a circular little sheet of water, now known as Turnbull's Bay. On either side the high shell bluffs were crowned with enormous live oaks, and beneath these the ground was clear of underbrush like a park, while beyond could be seen the rich green of a large wild orange grove, famous among the Indians for generations. Magnolias and green bay trees added graceful variety to the scene. This is the description by the famous naturalist, William Bartram, of the site of New Smyrna, which he visited ten years before the settlement was made.[2] Bartram's

---

(1) C.O. 5/544 pp. 37-42.
(2) Bartram's Travels, p. 142.

DR. ANDREW TURNBULL

young son dreamed of this spot for eighteen years after he saw it with his father, and returned to it when he had earned enough money in the Northern colonies to allow him to travel. The beauty and very apparent fertility of the place completely won Turnbull, and he decided to spend his life and risk his fortune in this garden forest. Although a physician, the name "Mosquito Inlet" held no warning for him, because science did not then connect the mosquito with the deadly malarial fevers which, in the next eight years, were to reduce this colony to half its original number. Moreover it was not until summer that he saw his people black with them as they worked at clearing the dense palmetto and vine-tied thickets, and found himself helpless without our modern methods of exterminating these pests, common to the whole Atlantic coast. Life promised much to the pioneer doctor and, in honor of his wife's birthplace, Smyrna, in Asia Minor, and in anticipation of his Greek settlers, he named the future settlement New Smyrna.

Turnbull was so impressed with the agricultural prospects of Florida that before he returned to England he purchased a large cotton plantation at the Mosquitoes and left an overseer in charge, with orders to buy cattle from Georgia and Carolina.[1] By the last of March, 1767, however, he was back in England, and presented his petition to make a settlement in Florida.[2] In his first grant from the crown there had been included twenty thousand acres for himself. Five subsequent grants to Duncan, Grenville and Turnbull, brought their whole tract to 101,400 acres.[3] Lord Grenville, at this time head of the ministry in England, was inclined to favor agricultural enterprises such as this, not only because he was Turnbull's partner, but in order to off-

---

(1) Lansdowne Ms. Vol. 88 f. 133.
(2) C.O. 5/223 Vol. lettered Board of Trade No. 1.
(3) Treasury 77/7, Memorial of Thomas Grenville, Esq.

DR. ANDREW TURNBULL

set the severity of his measures against smuggling in the colonies. The Lords of Trade granted Turnbull's request for a sloop of war to be used as a transport, and the forty-five hundred pounds of bounty on East Florida products was represented by the young Lord Shelburne, secretary for the colonies, as necessary for starting the settlement. Four hundred pounds was to be used for roads, bridges and ferries, one hundred pounds for a "Parson and Schoolmaster" and three pounds apiece for the cost of transportation of each colonist to the settlement.[1] It is, therefore, evident that the English government was as much interested in this undertaking as any shareholder in the Company. It also continued to give substantial assistance for at least four years thereafter.

---

(1) C.O. 5/563 p. 226-228; Lords of Trade to Shelburne.

CHAPTER II

THE MAKING OF NEW SMYRNA

EARLY in the Spring of 1767, Turnbull set sail in his converted sloop to collect settlers from Greece. This vessel was manned and provisioned by Turnbull himself,[1] no small investment for one individual in those days of slow travel, and as he proceeded to gather his colonists, his fleet grew to considerable size. He had difficulty, however, in persuading the Greeks to emigrate because the Turkish Government opposed his scheme.[2] Nevertheless he secured two hundred wild

---

(1) Lansdowne, Vol. 88 f. 133.

(2) Landsdowne Mss. Vol. 88 f. 147.

tribesmen from the mountains in the southernmost part of the Peloponnesus, who had always defied Turkish rule and who lived under chiefs in a state of civil war, when they were not fighting the Turks. These recruits did not produce a favorable impression on the Ottoman empire and when Turnbull sent a ship's crew ashore for water at Modon in the Morea, the commander of the garrison seized them as rebels. This officer was prevailed upon by presents to release them, but everywhere the Turks placed obstacles in the way of the enterprise.[1]

Finally Turnbull decided to go to Leghorn in Southern Italy for recruits, for the Governor there agreed to allow Italians to sign contracts with him, on condition that he take no Genoese silk manufacturers.[2] One hundred and ten Italians joined the expedition, but

---

(1) Lansdowne Ms. Vol. 88 f. 147.

(2) Lansdowne Ms. Vol. 88 f. 135.

when the governor saw that he was really about to lose these men, he sent many threatening messages to them. The British consul aided Turnbull in getting away with them, however,[1] and the Italians themselves told Turnbull that the majority of them were unemployed and strangers in the city of Leghorn, and therefore liable to deportation at any time. His agreement with the settlers was, that they were to have their way paid and to be established on the Florida grant. After they had paid off their indebtedness to the Company by from seven to eight years' labor, each was to receive fifty acres of land, with five additional acres for each child in his family.[2] If they were not contented with the land, they were to be allowed to return to their own country in six months.[2]

While Turnbull was having difficulty in persuading settlers to emigrate to Florida, news

---

(1) Lansdowne Ms. Vol. 88 f. 135.

(2) Schoepf, pp. 233-236.

reached him that crops in the island of Minorca had failed for the third consecutive year and that a large part of the farming population was on the verge of starvation. It seemed to him that these were the people who would join in an agricultural enterprise in a country that promised rich soil and plenty of land. Minorca had been an English possession since 1713, so it would not involve any bargaining with a foreign government or cause his colonists any uneasiness, such as might be occasioned by a change of allegiance. Although there was widespread discontent there, on account of England's policy of restricting the correspondence and activities of the Catholic priests of Minorca, she had promised Spain to allow them the freedom of their faith. She did not keep her treaty promises of freedom of religion in Minorca or Florida as she did in Canada, however. In proof of this, one condition of Turnbull's grants from the crown was that the settlers were all to be Protestants.[1] When Turn-

---

(1) C.O. 5/548 pp. 363-365.

THE NEW SMYRNA COLONY OF FLORIDA

bull first received his grant, this did not promise to be a difficulty, for the original plan had been to obtain Greeks, and since the Greek Catholic Church has always been regarded by the Church of England as an affiliation, their church was not antagonistic to the Protestant provision of the grants. But Minorcans, though English subjects, were Roman Catholics, and if they were to be colonists, their religion had to be ignored, as had been done in the other English colonies, Maryland excepted. Still, Turnbull argued, the situation did not promise to be any more acute in one colony of England, such as Minorca or Virginia, than in another, namely Florida. So when he decided to enlist the Minorcans, he allowed them to take a priest and monk with them, with letters and credentials from the Vicar General of Minorca.[1]

The island of Minorca lies among a flock of sister islands under the lee of Spain in the

---

(1) Unwritten History of St. Augustine, p. 222.

DR. ANDREW TURNBULL

Mediterranean. Its inhabitants are of Spanish extraction and appearance, speak a language similar to Spanish, and are devout Catholics. Most of them belong to the farming class, and, usually, they are sober, industrious and law-abiding, as Governor Grant testified when he expressly stated that they refused, to a man, to join the riots of Greeks and Italians which broke out the year the colony was started.[1]

In Minorca, Turnbull's project succeeded like wildfire. Crowds of starving people thronged the decks as soon as his ships dropped anchor in Port Mahon, the capital of Minorca under English rule, and one of the finest harbors in the Mediterranean.[2] They begged him to take three times as many of them as he had planned, because they were in such pitiable condition that their Bishop had even been obliged to dispense them from the Ecclesiastical law of fast and abstinence.[3]

---

(1) C.O. 5/544 pp. 37-42, Grant to Hillsborough.
(2) Encyclopedia Britannica, Vol. XVIII, p. 554.
(3) Unwritten History of St. Augustine, p. 202.

THE NEW SMYRNA COLONY OF FLORIDA

Now, there was another clause of Turnbull's grant which made him eager for as many settlers as possible. It provided that if one-third of his land was not settled in three years, in the proportion of one person to every hundred acres, the whole should be forfeited to the Crown, and that if the remainder was not so settled in ten years, it was likewise to be forfeited.[1] Therefore, he was delighted rather than daunted by the increasing size of his colony, and gave his approval when many of the Italians in the expedition married Minorcan girls, who were thus recruited for the colony.[2] Turnbull had already enough land in the Company's name for six hundred people and was planning for more grants, so he at once proceeded to enlarge his fleet to eight ships. The enormous increase in the expense of the undertaking seemed to him to be worth the risk, since he had complete Government

---

(1) C.O. 5/548, p. 363-365, Land Grant to Turnbull.

(2) Lansdowne Ms. Vol. 88, fo. 133.

support. Lord Hillsborough, successor to Lord Shelburne in charge of the colonies, was indeed delighted when he heard of the sudden increase in numbers, calling it a "Noble addition" to Florida's settlement.[1] Turnbull, however, had yet to learn that one may have too much, even of such a good thing, as will develop later. By March 10, 1768, a letter from Hillsborough to the Governor of Florida informed him that Turnbull had finally sailed from Minorca.[2]

Thus Turnbull scoured the Mediterranean for recruits, and collected a heterogeneous company—unruly Greek tribesmen of a strange language and different religion from the others, devout Roman Catholic farmers and a small but turbulent band of Italians. Being on the ground, Turnbull saw a great opportunity for England's colonies in these settlers. His vision was very large and he wrote that

---

(1) C.O. 5/549, p. 81, Hillsborough to Grant.
(2) C.O. 5/549, Hillsborough to Grant.

THE NEW SMYRNA COLONY OF FLORIDA

many thousands of Italians and Greeks could be sent to America if the ships could be obtained to recruit them. Governor Grant, looking upon the practical aspect of this one colony, humorously declared, "I flatter myself I shall be able to keep them (the Indians) quiet—but to prevent the Greeks, Italians and Mahonese[1] from doing mischief * * * * to themselves" he considered a harder problem.[2]

This farsighted official, on hearing that Minorcans were among the colonists, called the Indians in the vicinity of New Smyrna together, and explained to them, "that the people at the Mosquitoes[3] were not the English but that they were Subjects to the Great King—that they lived upon a little Island in a warm climate—that they had been oppressed by the Spaniards and hated them, and had come here to help their Brothers, the English."[2] In this way, Grant tried

---

(1) Minorcans.
(2) C.O. 5/544, pp. 37-42, Grant to Hillsborough.
(3) The vicinity of New Smyrna was known as the "Mosquitoes" because of Mosquito Inlet, the outlet of the North Indian River.

DR. ANDREW TURNBULL

to keep the Indians from avenging hundreds of years of Spanish cruelty upon the people who so closely resembled them. He was partially successful, in spite of the fact that the government was slow to build a fort to protect the colony. After he left the country, the Indians were loosed on these unfortunate people by Turnbull's political enemies, so that it is small wonder that they found life unsupportable at Mosquito.

When the colonists at length left Gibraltar and started for the open Atlantic, there were about fifteen hundred souls in all, divided among the eight ships.[1] This was the largest colony at its start that had ever come to the New World.[2] The Virginia colony at Jamestown did not exceed five hundred people at any

---

(1) C.O. 5/541, p. 427. The names of the ships and number of colonists in each were as follows:

Charming Betsy	232	New Fortune	226
Henry and Carolina	142	Hope	150
Elizabeth	190	American Soldier	145
Friendship	198	Betsy	120
		Men, women and children	1403

(2) C.O. 5/541, pp. 423-424 Grant to Hillsborough.

time until it passed from a proprietary to a royal government; and it took the Massachusetts colony seven years to work up to fifteen hundred people.

In addition to the settlers, the ships carried "cotton gins for the cleaning of cotton and other models of engines of agriculture,"[1] and the carefully packed cuttings for grapes, olives and mulberries. A realization of the magnitude of his undertaking did not daunt Turnbull. He wrote to Lord Shelburne when he sailed: "Though I have heard, My Lord, that America is now separated from your Department, as your Lordship's assistance and encouragement engaged me to enter into the colonizing scheme in a much larger way than I at first intended, I will trouble you now and again with an account of how my little colony goes on."[2]

The British frigate Carysfort agreed to act

---

(1) Lans. Ms. Vol. 88 f. 147.
(2) Lans. Ms. Vol. 88, f. 147.

DR. ANDREW TURNBULL

as convoy for the transports to Gibraltar, to protect them from the Barbary pirates,[1] and they intended to start on March 29, 1767, but at the last minute Turnbull found that instead of losing colonists by desertion as he had expected, he had more than he could carry, on account of the eager enlistment of the Minorcans.[2] Luckily he secured a Danish ship to carry his overflow as far as Gibraltar and, since it could not go further, hired two small English vessels for the journey overseas.

At Gibraltar, the Earl of Shelburne's recommendations secured Turnbull every attention, and Commodore Spry ordered the Carysfort to convoy his eight vessels, full of colonists, as far as the Madeiras, because reports had come in of raids by Algerian pirates upon Dutch and French shipping.

The English government rightly considered

---

(1) Lans. Ms. Vol. 88, f. 151.

(2) Lans. Ms. Vol. 88, f. 145.

THE NEW SMYRNA COLONY OF FLORIDA

this a most important and promising enterprise, and for a time at least gave it all the assistance possible. Florida bade fair to catch up with the other colonies in giant strides. To readers today, it will seem incredible that an undertaking of this magnitude should have been launched the very year the Stamp Act was repealed—that wealthy men and statesmen would have invested their own and the Government's money in a colony while open rebellion and clashes with the government officials over the rigid enforcement of smuggling penalties were spreading in every English colony in America. It is indeed a far cry from present day investments, which rise and fall like a barometer in response to the changes in the political atmosphere. English statesmen were very ignorant and indifferent to American public opinion, even upon such a stirring subject as the Stamp Act. "There was not the smallest evidence that either Pitt or Cumberland, or any of the other statesmen who were concerned with the negotiation, were conscious that any serious question was impending in America."[1] It attracted so little attention that it was not until three years after the enactment of the Stamp Act that the new Ministry (Rockingham Cabinet) learned the views of Pitt on the subject; it was probably a surprise to them to learn that it had brought the colonies to the verge of open rebellion.[1] Revolutionary troubles did indeed travel slowly to Florida, for the colony lived eight years under Governor Grant, undisturbed by the uproar to the North, and Florida, like Canada, kept out of the Revolution, but the separation of the other colonies from England finally cut Florida adrift from her also.

As yet, the new settlers were only crowds of anxious sea-farers, however, and the business of being a pioneer proved to be a stern one from the very first, for many old and feeble people died during the voyage. Twenty-eight are said to have been buried at sea from one

---

(1) Lecky, Vol. III, p. 361.

vessel alone. The voyage lasted four months, despite the fact that the best season of the year was selected for those waters—springtime, when the storms of the fall and winter were past, and the sweltering calms of summer were yet to come. Nevertheless, in the tossing sailing vessels, the colonists suffered torments, mental as well as physical, through anxiety for what their future might be, and homesickness for the lands they would never see again. Turnbull noted this homesickness and afterwards sought to divert their minds from the old lands. He declared himself reluctant to cultivate vines and olives in Florida because he feared it would fill his colonists with sad memories,—yet he knew that the Greeks had nothing to hope for from their former Turkish masters, that the Italians had told him he saved them from being deported from Leghorn, and the Minorcans said he had brought them from an overcrowded, impoverished island.

The latter part of June, four vessels arrived

at St. Augustine, the other four having fallen a little to the north. "They dropt in slowly," wrote Governor Grant, "but all of them got safe to this Port."[1] The Spanish houses, and general plan of St. Augustine were a pleasing sight to the Latin portion of the immigrants, and they remembered the close walled town throughout their residence in New Smyrna, and, after eight years, returned to it in a body, to live under its friendly shelter. At this time, however, they were dispatched at once by land and water to the Mosquitoes, to prepare for the other settlers who were delayed. As always happens when a large and elaborate plan approaches its culmination, many important phases went wrong. A ship containing five hundred negroes, who had been purchased and brought direct from Africa to clear the land and do the first rough work of the settlement, was wrecked on the southern coast of Florida, and all hands were lost.[2]

---

(1) C.O. 5/544, pp. 37-42, Grant to Hillsborough.
(2) Schoepf, pp. 233-236.

THE NEW SMYRNA COLONY OF FLORIDA

Strenuous measures were necessary to take care of such a great company of people, suddenly set down in a wild country. Governor Grant had had four months provisions placed there[1] and some great shacks erected for living quarters,[2] but the families were crowded for shelter and sleeping during the first weeks of organization, for, since nearly three times as many people had come as were expected, they were not prepared for them. Hominy was cooked in huge copper kettles in the open, and at meal time a drum summoned the workers from the woods to line up for their share of food. Clothes by the wholesale, of heavy durable material, and mostly of uniform pattern, were distributed, so as to save the colonists what was left of their wardrobes. Most of them were badly off, in the first place, so far as clothes were concerned, and this, therefore, was a much needed measure. Strange to say, however, all of these ways of

---

(1) C.O. 5/549, p. 49, Grant to Hillsborough.

(2) C.O. 5/549, pp. 77-78.

DR. ANDREW TURNBULL

caring for the settlers were mentioned as great grievances by their historian, Romans. This was the accepted way of providing for people in new colonies, the way that the Virginia, Georgia, Plymouth and Carolina colonists had lived for the first years of their pioneer life, but these people are reported to have been disappointed because they encountered these hardships.

Governor Grant gives a more favorable report of them, however. He says that by August 10, 1768, they were all located on plantations, appeared contented and pleased with their prospects and were obedient to their overseers.[1] In the directing of so many people for a division of labor and for information on their needs and progress, overseers were selected, partly from their own number and partly imported from the Northern colonies, the latter because of their knowledge of New World agriculture. Many of the colonists

---

(1) C.O. 5/544, pp. 37-42, Grant to Hillsborough.

were entirely ignorant of the methods of clearing and planting, all of them had to learn how to raise hemp, cotton and indigo, the articles on which England had placed a bounty. But these English overseers came from plantations where negroes had been used as laborers and, in addition to being unable to understand the language of their Minorcan, Italian and Greek charges, they made themselves unpopular by their arbitrary manner and impatience at what they claimed was the stupidity and laziness of some of the settlers. Also, the colonists had all come, as generations before and after them, with dreams of ease and plenty to be enjoyed without work in Florida. So it was not long before peremptory commands and the strict discipline necessary to preserve order in the new colony brought about a clash between the unruly element and their directors.

Van de Sande Studio, New Smyrna, Fla.

ONE OF THE MANY COQUINA-LINED WELLS AT NEW SMYRNA

CHAPTER III

THE UPRISING OF 1768[1]

ALL seemed peaceful and busy on August 8, 1768, two months after the last colonist had arrived at New Smyrna, when Turnbull brought some planters from the Carolinas down to see the progress his settlers had made. The distinguished visitors rode over the fields where brush and pine stumps were burning, the fresh-cut outlines of the farms were just showing and the great wharfs and wells were being built of coquina. Turnbull showed them

---

(1) C.O. 5/544, pp. 37-42.
    (This account is based upon Governor Grant's report to Hillsborough and the Lords of Trade of the occurrence).

DR. ANDREW TURNBULL

the quarries of this curious rock which is composed of innumerable tiny shells, held together by a natural cement, a rough and durable material which the Spaniards had used to build the fort and sea-wall at St. Augustine. The colonists were much awed by the splendid equipment and retinue with which these visitors traveled, but the visitors were equally impressed by the extent of the undertaking before them. They saw that this was the largest number of people which had ever come to the colonies in one body; that the possibilities of the country were at last to be found in agriculture, instead of myths of gold and silver, and that within his grasp Turnbull held the realization of all the visions of past invaders of this strange land. They declared to their delighted host that this colony bade fair to be "the best in all the British provinces," and added that their own experienced laborers could not have done better than these people in preparing the plantations.

That day the distinguished company rode

on its way to St. Augustine, accompanied by Dr. Turnbull, and stopped for the night at Mt. Oswald, the large sugar cane plantation on the Halifax River. The natural surroundings of this country seat are today the wonder and delight of tourists at Daytona and Ormond. But how different was life there then! These planters lived on their huge land grants, surrounded by slaves and in danger of Indians. They could only reach St. Augustine by rough corduroy roads or a sail down the coast, with the possibility of being captured by pirates, and they were now about to be treated to a new realization of the vicissitudes of pioneer life. On the night of the 19th, they sat around the great hall in Mr. Oswald's home, resting from their tour of inspection, until about ten o'clock, when they retired, in order to be ready to start on their way to St. Augustine the next morning. At midnight an express rider dashed up to the quiet house and hammered on the door, calling for Dr. Turnbull. Candles were hurriedly lit by the house servants and the distracted messenger admitted to the doctor's room, where he delivered himself of a tale of black calamity. It seemed that Carlo Forni, one of the Italian overseers, that very morning, about eleven o'clock, had marched into the square, at New Smyrna, at the head of twenty malcontents, and delivered a speech to the settlers, who left their work and crowded around the storehouse to hear him. He declared himself commander-in-chief of the Italians and Greeks, whom he intended to lead to Havana. Spain, he argued, would be glad to protect them from the English, and they would be freed from this life of hard work and stern masters. The sandy, desolate shores of Florida held nothing but sickness and danger for them and he was prepared to deliver them from all their troubles. As he talked, the crowd grew excited. Clotha Corona, one of his Greek followers, broke the door of the storehouse and casks of rum were rolled into the street. At this moment, Cutter, one of the English overseers, arrived on the scene and tried to order the crowd away. He was wounded in the struggle with Forni's men and locked in one of the closets of the storeroom. Excited with this violence and by the rum, which was now circulating freely in the mob, the adherents of Froni rapidly increased until they numbered about three hundred. They seized firearms and ammunition in the storehouse and compelled the Minorcans to submit to their commands, though the latter refused to a man to join the rioting. For this, their dwellings were plundered and their belongings thrown into the road. But other and richer prizes soon diverted the mob. A ship of provisions, lying in the river, was seized, and the work of loading her for the trip to Cuba commenced. Clothes, blankets, linen and fishing tackle were carried down to the shore by the hundreds of armfuls, and the rum and oil casks which could not be loaded were staved in in the streets. The number of men actively implicated included nearly all the Greeks and Italians in the colony, and Carlo Forni threatened that anyone who tried to escape and warn the authorities would be put to death. Nevertheless, two faithful Italians slipped into the swamp at dusk and made their way to Turnbull's plantation, four miles from New Smyrna. There was no one but the overseer in charge here and their terrified version of the course of events, as delivered to him, sounded like the end of New Smyrna's young settlement. So he sent an "express" rider through the woods that very evening, and this was the story that had reached the doctor at midnight and dashed his high hopes for his model settlement. As he sat and listened, he saw one hundred and sixty thousand dollars, which included his own fortune, and the money of his powerful friends, sunk in a community of violent and unprincipled men. Two years of hard preparatory work gone, extensive plans half executed, and himself a ruined man. But he roused himself at once, and thanked God that his wife and children were still in St. Augustine, waiting the completion of their new home. He dismissed the messenger for rest and refreshment, and sat down at once to write Governor Grant a full account of what had happened. He asked that help be sent him at once to New Smyrna, where he was returning that very night in the hope of checking the uprising. And, in the small hours of the morning, another express rider started at top speed for St. Augustine, while Turnbull bade goodbye to his friends and former guests, and set his face toward New Smyrna.

He arrived at his plantation some time in the morning of the 20th, and at once started, with a small company of servants, to rescue his wounded overseer. The marauders were down at the waterfront, loading their spoils, and the terrified Minorcans were hiding in their quarters, so he went down the littered street to the storehouse without interruption. Cutter was soon located and brought out—one of his ears and two fingers had been cut off and continued bleeding and severe handling had reduced him to a serious condition. All other considerations faded before the need for the services of a doctor, and so Turnbull had Cutter carried back to the plantation, where he treated his wounds and cared for him, while waiting for word from the Governor.

The next day passed without events of any moment. Messengers from New Smyrna reported to Turnbull that the mutineers did not seem to be hurrying to leave, that they were feasting and drinking aboard their ship most of the night and had not yet finished loading. Cutter was very ill all day and required constant attention, raving at his imagined assailants. The night came, and with it word that the rebel ship would sail on the morning's tide, so it was an anxious vigil for the doctor. Early in the morning, he rode over to the shore and mournfully watched the sails go up on the crowded vessel, as it moved down the river and out of sight, to anchor at the bar and wait for the eleven o'clock tide. The loss of three hundred able-bodied men out of the colony was a staggering blow, not to mention thou-

THE NEW SMYRNA COLONY OF FLORIDA

sands of dollars worth of supplies and the ship. He turned his horse and rode slowly along the bank toward Mosquito Inlet. Suddenly, within a mile of the bar, he heard a gun fired and his heart leaped with excitement and renewed hope. He dashed along the shore and reached the Inlet in time to see the East Florida, with another vessel behind her, sail down upon the escaping ship, on the very tide which was to have carried her off to Cuba. The rebel's deck was swarming with terrified men who waved white rags and showed that they were ready to surrender. Before the government ships could get to her, however, Turnbull saw about thirty-five men escape in an open boat and row frantically around the wooded shore. A few hours later, he met the officer in charge of the relief expedition at the wharf, and watched with immense relief the unloading of his property by the frightened mutineers, who had been deserted by their leader and his accomplices. They eagerly obeyed the soldiers in charge of them. In

DR. ANDREW TURNBULL

talking with the captain, he heard how Grant had received his letter the evening of the day he had sent it, had loaded his ships all night long and sent them out on the 21st. Two days sail had completed their journey and brought them to New Smyrna in the nick of time. Turnbull felt very happy at this moment; realizing that most of these mutineers were like simple sheep following a few ringleaders as blundering as they were lawless, he recommended that only a few of the most guilty be taken to St. Augustine for trial. Inquiry among the insurgents proved that they were as enraged with their leaders on account of their desertion, as Turnbull was for their lawlessness.

As soon as things were quiet again, and Turnbull was sure that a small guard could maintain order in the colony, the relief expedition sent one ship in search of the ringleaders, whom they expected to catch easily, while the other returned to St. Augustine. A strange chase for the escaped men took place down the long open coast. It was four months before the government ship overtook them on the Florida Keys, and then it is probable that their dreadful hardships had made them anxious to be caught. All through the Fall season of terrible northeast storms, these thirty-five men had traveled in an open boat along the shore, camping and hunting sometimes, not daring to stay long on land for fear of Indians and wild beasts, or long on water because of storms and their pursuers. It is small wonder that their wretched appearance moved the jurors in St. Augustine to pity. Governor Grant himself wrote to the Earl of Hillsborough that he thought the men had been punished enough by their experience, and that justice dealt to two or three flagrant offenders would be sufficient for the whole three hundred. So three were finally convicted of piracy, and one of these pardoned on a curiously cruel condition—that he be the executioner of the other two. (English law was still very severe in those days—there is a

DR. ANDREW TURNBULL

petition from the Governor of Massachusetts about this time, asking that the death penalty for forgery be changed). The two men who were executed were Carlo Forni, guilty of leading the insurrection, and the man who was responsible for the death of Cutter, who had since succumbed to his wounds. Three Greeks, convicted of less violent crimes, were pardoned by Grant on the recommendation of Hillsborough. Turnbull estimated his losses, after affairs had settled down, at four or five hundred pounds. In the light of the English law of the day and its heavy penalties, the offenders at New Smyrna were certainly gently dealt with, just as all wise and enlightened authorities usually manage a large number of lawbreakers. The whole three hundred of them were guilty of piracy; but their future good conduct was assured by lenient measures.

All previous accounts of this uprising have been based upon Bernard Romans' version, which he included in his "History of Florida," on the authority of his irresponsible youthful draughtsman. All subsequent historians are unanimous in pronouncing Romans' History as lurid and unreliable, yet they took his word for a most barbarous recital of cruelty on Turnbull's part, and none of them consulted the detailed report of this affair by the governor of the province to the British Secretary of State, surely a most sane and authoritative source of information, and the one on which this account is based.[1]

Yet we may surely draw our own conclusions from the course of events themselves. The leaders of the revolt could not have had the welfare of the whole community at heart, for they planned to leave New Smyrna in a ship which had a capacity of not more than one-fifth of the people, and they destroyed the provisions they could not take with them. Also, they were not even capable of effecting their own escape, but spent three days in rioting and drinking—enough time for two govern-

(1) C.O. 5/544, Grant to Hillsborough, pp. 37-42.

ment ships to load troops and make the journey from St. Augustine. So this rebellion was nothing more than the haphazard rioting of lawless men who used rum and vain promises to lead their unthinking companions into mischief.

Governor Grant summed up the affair by saying it was to be expected that a large number of people imported from all parts of the world to a new country would have such troubles; and he ended his report by recommending that a fort be built at New Smyrna for the double purpose of protecting the settlers from the Indians and of protecting the other planters from the settlers.[1] Already, he said, the plantations around New Smyrna were the most prosperous in Florida, and deserved the utmost care from the Government. A fort was accordingly started but never finished, though a guard of a sergeant and eight men was stationed there permanently.[2]

---

(1) C.O. 5/544, pp. 37-42.
(2) C.O. 5/552, p. 97-99.

de Sande Studio, New Smyrna, Fla.
FOUNDATIONS OF THE FORT WHICH WAS NEVER FINISHED, NEW SMYRNA

CHAPTER IV

ENGLAND LENDS FINANCIAL AID

BY December 1st, Grant wrote the home Government that the Greeks and Italians were quiet, but that scurvey had broken out, as a result of their long sea voyage and the scarcity of fresh foods at that season of the year; so that the settlement had lost about three hundred old people and children from sickness.[1] The remedy of green vegetables and fruits was not far off, however, for, he said, the gardens of that vicinity were about as far advanced as they were in England by the end of April and, with a touch of plant-

---

(1) C.O. 5/544, pp. 99-102, Grant to Hillsborough.

DR. ANDREW TURNBULL

er's pride, "I took care to save a considerable quantity (of seeds) for Mr. Turnbull from my own garden, of which a grain does not fail here."

A clear statement of coming financial troubles occurs in this same letter which Grant wrote to the Earl of Hillsborough, the new Secretary for the colonies. "Twenty thousand pounds sterling * * * have already been laid out for the Embarkation, Provisions and Clothing of those people." Certainly this does not sound like an illiberal scale so far. He continued, "So large a Sum is not to be recovered but by perseverance and a further Expense, the settlers may do a little for themselves in the course of the Winter and Spring, but they must be subsisted for many months and clothed at least for two years before Returns can reasonably be expected—though they are supplied with Economy and good management—I am much afraid that the Expense of supporting so large a Settlement will

THE NEW SMYRNA COLONY OF FLORIDA

be found too considerable for private pockets.[1] I give Mr. Turnbull every little assistance in my power, and I can safely say that I am as anxious about his success as he can be himself; but unless your Lordship is pleased to take this Greek Settlement under your Protection and include it in the Estimate for 1769, I am apprehensive that Mr. Turnbull will find great difficulty in carrying the projected plan into Execution—it is upon a larger bottom than was concerted with his Friends at home, and has already far exceeded double the Sum which they agreed to advance, for which reason, My Lord, I am under some uneasiness about the future Conduct of those Gentlemen, they may probably tire of paying the large and frequent Bills, which Mr. Turnbull is under the absolute necessity of drawing upon them—their affairs certainly could not be in better hands, the Doctor is active, intelligent and assidu-

---

[1] This is the difficulty in a nutshell—the same difficulty which caused the other British colonies to be taken from their companies by the Crown.

ous—but his Friends, tho' they have the highest opinion of Mr. Turnbull's integrity and Ability may possibly be alarmed at risking such large sums in a New World without a more immediate prospect of Returns for their Money—what I now mention to your Lordship is entirely from my private opinion for I am sure the Doctor is convinced of my Friendship and good wishes—I cannot help considering the dreadful situation which the Doctor and his Greeks would be reduced to, if such a misfortune was to happen, a single Bill being returned, My Lord, would put a total stop to his Credit—in such a case of necessity I must run the risk, draw upon the Treasury for the subsistence of those adventurers and depend upon your Lordship's protection to support me in what I do—tho' this affair, My Lord, has hung heavy upon my mind, since the Landing of so great a number of people at a time, without any previous provision being made for them, and without the consent of the other parties concerned, as the

THE NEW SMYRNA COLONY OF FLORIDA

Mahonese crowded in unexpectedly upon Mr. Turnbull."[1]

Turnbull had six thousand pounds to start with, and the British Government had only promised him a bounty on the first five hundred colonists, so that the whole scale of his settlement was according to his expected five hundred people; but, when the hundreds of starving Minorcans had thronged the decks of his transports, and begged to be taken from their famine stricken land, his enthusiasm was aroused by the prospect of such a wonderful colony. It seemed reasonable to him to suppose that if five hundred settlers were eagerly welcomed to Florida, fourteen hundred would be even more acceptable, especially when they were of the much needed farming class. But he was beginning to learn that there were many fatal and inevitable complications awaiting him.

By the 4th of March, 1769, the health of the

---

(1) C.O. 5/544, pp. 99-102, Grant to Hillsborough.

DR. ANDREW TURNBULL

colonists had been restored and they had cleared seven miles of water front along the Hillsborough, now the North Indian River.[1] Each farm house was set 210 feet from the next along the river, with its allotted acreage running back, and Turnbull, whose Mediterranean travels had lasted over many years, wrote that they reminded him of Egyptian farms along the Nile.[2] Their gardens were well started and the drainage of the rich swamp lands was progressing in a thorough and scientific way. But the bills were pouring in now, and every time Turnbull had to send a ship for provisions and clothing he did not know whether payment on them would be stopped or not. To avoid drawing any more money, he would wait until the last possible moment to replenish his stores. Governor Grant understood his predicament perfectly and knew his reluctance to call upon his friends any further, but he would not allow him to

---

(1) C.O. 5/544, pp. 200-201, Grant to Hillsborough.
(2) Lansdowne Ms. Vol. 88, f. 155.

run too great a risk or depend on an exact date for a sailing vessel's arrival. "I have always recommended to him to have Six Months provisions constantly in store. Mr. Turnbull, just as I expected, finds himself, this moment very much pinched for provisions as his Supplies have not arrived exactly to the time and he writes that he has only Indian Corn for a Month at the Mosquitoes. I shall take care to prevent his being distressed, tho' I have no objection to his being a little uneasy," says the Governor humorously, "and therefore without telling him or anybody else, I have sent the "East Florida" to Charleston with directions to load her with Indian Corn, and with private orders to the Captain to proceed directly to New Smyrna, tho' I give out here that the Vessel is going to Savannah for Lumber."[1] So, even if Turnbull had allowed provisions to run low, this able Governor watched the colony too closely to allow it to suffer from hunger. In fact there appears to be ample

---

(1) C.O. 5/544, pp. 200-201, Grant to Hillsborough.

DR. ANDREW TURNBULL

proof of the care that was centered on these people.

Governor Grant's eloquent plea to Hillsborough of the worthiness of Dr. Turnbull's cause induced the Lords of the Treasury to allow him two thousand pounds for the support of the settlement, when further payments were stopped by the London Company, which, by July 21, 1769, had expended twenty-eight thousand pounds. Grant wrote to Hillsborough again, to tell him that the two thousand pounds would not be sufficient for the support of the colony, and urged that the East Florida bounty of five hundred pounds a year be continued for the benefit of New Smyrna.[1] It is evident that great pressure was brought to bear upon Dr. Turnbull to obtain returns for such an enormous outlay. Grant reported, September 1, 1770, "Dr. Turnbull is diligent and assiduous, he resides constantly with his Greek colonists and does as much as man can

---

(1) C.O. 5/544, pp. 213-214.

do, to repair the first fault of exceeding the number of people to be Imported."[1] The settlers raised a considerable amount of provisions, such as Indian corn, peas, potatoes and greens of all kinds, but the scarcity of money for the further work of the colony is evident from the rest of Grant's letter. "They are destitute of every convenience, they are ill clothed, many of them almost naked—and are obliged to live in small Huts put up in a hurry to shelter them from the Weather upon their first arrival. Dr. Turnbull has neither money nor credit to supply them with clothes and has not the necessary Tools and Materials to build Houses for them, in that distressed situation he can only look up to His Majesty for his most gracious support by ordering the Royal Bounty to be continued to enable him to carry an extensive and useful undertaking into Execution with Success—he presses me to lay his case before Your Lordship and to trans-

---

(1) C.O. 5/545, pp. 33-34.

DR. ANDREW TURNBULL

mit for Your Lordship's consideration an indent of such things as are absolutely necessary for the existence of the settlement."[1] This indent is interesting because it gives an idea of how extensive financially even a few items for the colony could be. It reads:

> "Indent of Clothing, Tools, etc., wanted for the Distressed Greek Settlement at Smyrna, under the direction of Andrew Turnbull, Esq.,
>
> Best blue plains—3000 yards at ¼ s per yard..200 pounds
> Best white plains—500 yards at ¼ s per yard 33. 6. 8
> Check't Linnens—3000 yards at 1- per yard..150
> Strip't Linnens—2000 yards at 1- per yard..100
> Strip't Cottons—500 yards at ⅓ d per yard.. 31. 5
> Scots Osnabruggs[2] 4000 yards at 6 d per yard 100
> Negro Blankets—600 at 5s each............150
> Men's shoes of different sizes—600 pr at
>   ¾ d per pair..........100
> Indigo Sickles 60 doz'n at 8/6 d per Dozen.. 25. 10
> Broad Hoes, Crowley's of a middling size
>   60 Dozen at 20/ per Dozen.... 60
> Building nails the greatest part Six penny..100
>
>   Lbs 1050. 18

Another shortage of provisions in October, 1770, was caused by Carolina planters who

---

(1) C.O. 5/545, pp. 33-34.
(2) A coarse kind of linen.

sold their promised cargo to a Spanish vessel, instead of sending it to New Smyrna. A substitute cargo was secured by Grant, however.

While Grant was trying to help him with the Government, Turnbull had made a new arrangement with his partners, to meet the increased scale of his settlement.[1] On October 2, 1769, Duncan and Temple agreed to pay 24,000 pounds on the colony if the shares in the property were divided into fifths, giving them each two-fifths and Turnbull one, in the final dividends. Thus Turnbull lost his one-third share in the company by increasing the expense of the undertaking. He lost land principally, for all further grants he obtained were still to be divided into fifths for the Company. Grenville incidentally advised him to look out for Indian lands, that is, land the Indians were willing to sell. But Turnbull was too busy to do this for several years.

These were some of the difficulties which

---

(1) T. 77/7, Second Indenture.

harassed the administrator at New Smyrna, of which the colonists had no idea. They prospered for the most part in a rough, backwoods way, and their hardships were not to be compared with the sufferings of the earlier colonists of North America. They had a mild climate, soil of wonderful fertility, and a river abounding in fish, oysters and turtles. Game was also plentiful, and while the Indians troubled them, it was as thieves and not as murderers. Still, sickness continued to reduce their numbers and the occasional shortage of clothes, food or tools caused by Turnbull's recalcitrant London partners caused grumblings, which centered on Turnbull himself. He was the only organizer they knew anything about, and him they held responsible for all things, good or bad, which happened to them.

CHAPTER V

GOVERNOR GRANT LEAVES FLORIDA

IN the brief accounts of this colony there has been room only for the troubles that assailed it on all sides, so that its five or six years of remarkable progress are passed over with little comment. William Bartram, in his famous "Travels Through the Southern Provinces," commented on the pretty, thriving town on the west bank of the North Indian River; Johann Schoepf, a German traveler, also described its plantations extending for miles along the banks, the palmetto cottages of the settlers forming the picturesque center of each family's allotted acreage. The colony grew the necessities of

DR. ANDREW TURNBULL

life first—maize, sugar, cotton and rice, which they shipped from their great coquina wharfs. They also gathered sea weed and burned it for barilla, the ash of which makes sodium carbonate of an impure sort. Indigo, too, proved very successful, and they dug huge vats in the fields for boiling it. At the end of the first year, Turnbull was able to dispose of five thousand bushels of corn, after the supply for the colony had been deducted; while in 1772 the shipment of indigo brought them three thousand pounds,[1] a sum which, of course, meant more then than it does now. Mulberry trees for silkworms were planted and grapevines set out. Turnbull also imported cochineal insects for making scarlet dye. These insects may still be seen, clinging in white webs to the cactus plants in the woods about New Smyrna.

With the dawning era of success for the

---

[1] Treasury 77/7. Statement of London merchant who credited the colony with this sum to barter.

colony, Turnbull became a leader in the new province. He had been made a member of the East Florida Council, May 13, 1767, that is, as soon as it was definitely known that he would live in Florida. Grant had written, October 20, 1768, that the management of New Smyrna consumed so much of Turnbull's time that he was unable to act as Clerk of the East Florida Council and Secretary of the Province, and a Mr. Yeats was temporarily performing these duties for him, but they remained his honorary posts.[1] He was so prominent and had made such a good impression on the home government that the Earl of Hillsborough began to urge his appointment as successor to Governor Grant,[2] when the latter was obliged, on account of failing health, to resign his office, in 1770. This resignation was a very disastrous event for the future of Florida and New Smyrna. Governor Grant, whose tireless care for this province had given it the

---

(1) C.O. 5/544, pp. 95-96.
(2) C.O. 5/545, pp. 60-61.

greatest era of prosperity in its long tragic history, was not only obliged to resign his office, but to leave Florida. By October 19, 1770, he had received his Majesty's license to return to England, but he did not go until the last of March, 1771, because he was needed in the colony. Two important questions occupied him—the selection of his successor, and the continuance of the bounty for the New Smyrna colony—and in both of them Turnbull was concerned. Hillsborough sent him a list of candidates for the governorship for him to pass upon, and he commented as follows:

> "Mr. Wooldridge would not do at all.
>
> Mr. Jolly—also objected to—
>
> "Mr. Turnbull, the third your Lordship mentions is unexceptionable, but his constant Residence at Smyrna is absolutely and indispensably necessary. Without his presence the business of the Settlement

could not go on. He and his Constituents have too much at Stake to neglect the Greek Colony which requires his attention. He is not to be thought of—I only count on him as an honorary Councellor, who I do not expect to see but once a year and that only for a day or two. When he came last from Smyrna, it was to pass some days at my Plantation to see the process of making Indigo, in which great Improvements have been made this year by my Manufacturies."[1]

Thus it is evident that Turnbull had to sacrifice everything to his colony—all governmental or professional honors which offered a wide field with few contestants in Florida. As he was one of the three doctors in East Florida he came in for that affection and respect from the people in the province which

---

(1) C.O. 5/545, pp. 60-61, Grant to Hillsborough.

DR. ANDREW TURNBULL

only a doctor can command. In spite of his remoteness from people he gained renown for his skill in treating the diseases of Southern countries.[1]

Hillsborough was still reluctant to give up his name for the governorship however, and Grant wrote again, "Doctor Turnbull obliged to constant Residence at Smyrna, could not with propriety think of entering into the Administration, if he was to be continued in it—and of course as things are Circumstanced will not interfere with Mr. Moultrie." John Moultrie was the man urged for the position by Grant, for he was one of the largest planters, owned the magnificent estate of Bella Vista, seven miles from St. Augustine, and moreover, "If he does not succeed to the Administration in my absence, we shall certainly lose him," concluded Grant. Hillsborough yielded to the extent of appointing Moultrie Lieutenant-Governor, but the opinion of the people in

---

[1] Obituary, Charleston City Gazette, Mar. 14, 1792.

the province persisted that Turnbull would soon be made Governor.[1]

While Grant prevented the appointment of Turnbull as Governor, he sought to make up for it by his constant concern for the much needed bounty for the next year. "Transmitting my Letter to the Board of Treasury, My Lord, will not procure the Bounty for the Greek Settlement, if my request is not supported by your Lordship's approbation of the Measure, which I think in the end would be attended with much Utility to the Publick—by enabling Dr. Turnbull to carry his extensive Plans into Execution, the Progress of which must be very slow, indeed the Subsistence of his People will be precarious if he is not better established, before the Royal Bounty is withdrawn."[2]

It has been shown what splendid support Grant had given the Turnbull settlement, and

---

(1) Forbes, p. 22.
(2) C.O. 5/545, pp. 81-82.

DR. ANDREW TURNBULL

how necessary the close co-operation of the Government had been for the bare existence of the colony, and so it can easily be imagined that even a luke-warm attitude by the administration would make matters very difficult at New Smyrna, while any opposition could easily send the costly undertaking into bankruptcy. By this time, George Grenville was dead, Shelburne out of favor and the Home Government much too engrossed in events in the North to listen to Florida's troubles. Early in the year the Boston Massacre had put the colonists into disfavor with the Home Government, and Hillsborough was not inclined to continue his benevolence, even toward New Smyrna. The large sums they had spent in Georgia on colonies had not repaid them for their efforts, and besides, the Government had never felt obligated to care for Turnbull's colony; they had only promised bounty for five hundred colonists; they had afterwards granted the two thousand pounds as a special relief measure, on condition that the Treasury should not be put to any more expense; and now, they flatly refused any more assistance. Grant drew Hillsborough's displeasure upon himself by his insistence on this bounty. "I have already acquainted you that I had communicated to the Lords of the Treasury the Request for a further Allowance for the Support of Dr. Turnbull's colony of Greeks."[1] But he had nothing to add to his former statement. "I cannot take upon me to authorize any further expense to the public on that Account." Henceforth New Smyrna had to shift for itself, and Turnbull to do the best he could to recover from the agricultural efforts of his colonists the great sums sunk in their undertaking.

---

(1) C.O. 5/545, pp. 289-290.

CHAPTER VI

THE NEW GOVERNOR

LIFE at New Smyrna proceeded uneventfully on the surface for a time. Mr. Frazier, the Protestant Minister at New Smyrna, died in 1772, and Moultrie wrote the Earl of Hillsborough that he had arranged for Mr. Forbes, the Minister at St. Augustine, to visit New Smyrna at intervals. Mrs. Turnbull, with her seven children, and her nephew, Andrew, presided in the Turnbull mansion, a large house, built of coquina, which stood about four miles from the settlement, and there Mr. Forbes was entertained, as were the prominent men who travelled to see the colony by sailing vessel or

DR. ANDREW TURNBULL

horseback. Grant had provided for the building of a splendid road to New Smyrna, which Moultrie continued. The roads built during the English occupation of Florida, are still called King's Roads, and show how well they were built, by their splendid lasting qualities. One ran from St. Augustine to New Smyrna, and another to Cowsford, (now Jacksonville) and thence to the St. Mary's River. There were many wealthy planters from the Carolinas and several noblemen from England who were the grantees of large tracts of land, among the latter, Lords Hauks, Egmont, Sir William Duncan and Messrs. Rolls, Oswald, Taylor, Bisset, Potts, Strachey, Tonyn and Turnbull.[1] Large plantations, with beautiful homes and groves were scattered over the vicinity of St. Augustine and New Smyrna and along the St. Johns River. There were now few unclaimed lands around New Smyrna. Turnbull's neighbors, as shown by the old sur-

---

(1) C.O. 5/546, pp. 227-228, Tonyn's letter to Germain.

THE NEW SMYRNA COLONY OF FLORIDA

vey maps,[1] were Messrs. Wright, Alortz, Samuel Campbell, Robert Paris Taylor, John Grayhurst, James Moultrie, Robert Oswald, Captain Samuel Barrington and Col. Wm. Faucet. Small holdings in the names of W. Waldron, T. Warron and Angus Clark filled in the long line of plantations. Bella Vista, the home of Lieutenant Governor Moultrie, was particularly famous for its beautiful grounds. The social center of all this prosperity was St. Augustine, and the little town was very gay under English administration.

As in all frontier posts, the brilliancy of the Governor's functions was furnished by the military. The officers of Fort George did not look favorably upon Moultrie's appointment, because they thought him lacking in force and decision, and, moreover, they were all staunch friends of Turnbull, whom they felt should have been made Governor. Chief Justice Drayton was another friend who now held aloof

---

(1) T. 77/7.

DR. ANDREW TURNBULL

from the official Mansion. He belonged to one of South Carolina's most prominent families, his grandfather and uncle both having been Lieutenant Governors there, and though Moultrie also came from South Carolina, the two had long been unfriendly. The attitude of the military was a source of irritation to Moultrie, and Turnbull he regarded with suspicion, but Drayton was the point of contact which set off the long train of explosive disagreements which finally led to New Smyrna's downfall. As has been said, Turnbull and Chief Justice Drayton were firm friends. They had long wished to see the governmental machinery, which England had provided for Florida, put in operation. The original letters patent of the Province had provided for a governor, council and elected assembly, but Grant had refused, throughout his administration, to allow the formation of the assembly. Turnbull had always disagreed with him on this subject, and, when Moultrie succeeded Grant, he and Drayton urged the election of an assembly, in the council meetings.[1] All parties in the council agreed that this was a good measure, since Florida had now enough people to merit a representative form of colonial government, but demonstrations against England in the Northern colonies, especially the clash between the inhabitants of Boston and British troops, in 1770, known as the Boston Massacre, had again alarmed the British ministry, and as there were, even in Florida, two parties on the question of the extent to which representative government should go at this time, much delay in this direction was experienced by the Florida colony. Florida was, in reality, too recently settled by the English and too evidently benefited by British rule to really wish for independence, but the King's party, with Moultrie at its head, advised elections to be held only once in three years, so as to control popular opinion, while Turnbull, Drayton and many other prominent men declared

---

(1) Forbes, p. 21.

DR. ANDREW TURNBULL

for annual elections. The same question was being agitated in England, from 1770-1771, where the Prime Minister, Chatham, was engaged in collecting opinion on the subject. Chatham favored annual elections, while Burke opposed them as lessening the power and prestige of Parliament.[1] As usual, Turnbull, who kept in touch with English politics, brought the latest question from England to Florida. The dispute on this subject between Drayton and Moultrie grew very heated, and finally extended to other matters, such as administrative and judicial business of the province, until these two gentlemen, "high-minded Carolinians," as Forbes terms them, were involved in an irremediable quarrel, Turnbull standing by the Chief Justice, both from conviction and friendship. The plan for an assembly failed entirely as a result, and Drayton resigned his seat in the council. Soon afterward, Turnbull resigned also; but

---

(1) Lecky, Vol. III, p. 361.

THE NEW SMYRNA COLONY OF FLORIDA

whether to show his affiliation with Drayton, or because he really was too busy to attend the meetings, Moultrie could not decide.[1] No further difference developed between Turnbull and Moultrie, however, for some years, probably because of the remoteness of New Smyrna from the capital. On February 19, 1773, Moultrie reported a visit which he had made to the Greek Colony, where he evidently found everything entirely satisfactory, for he wrote to the Earl of Dartmouth: "Since I last had the honor of addressing your Lordship, I have visited all the Plantations and Settlements on the Mosquito River, and I am happy to inform you that as well on this visitation as that of St. Johns River, I have reason to be pleased, and that a Spirit of Improvement, of Industry and good humor everywhere prevails among the Settlers; of which they feel the good effects. Their plantations carry the appearance of Improvement; they have plenty around

---

(1) C.O. 5./545, p. 289-290.

DR. ANDREW TURNBULL

them and are beginning to recover the expenses they have been at on their first setting down in this New Colony."[1] These are strange words for an official who, a little later, was to charge the orginator of this settlement with poor management and starving and maltreating his colonists; certainly he must have been blind to have seen on every plantation prosperity and good humor where hideous cruelty and famine were only a short time afterwards represented by him to prevail. In that day as well as now, politics played a large part in coloring the picture of existing conditions. Turnbull was well satisfied with the way the colony was prospering, for he wrote on October 3, 1774, "I have now laid a solid foundation, though it was against the opinion of some men, who prefer a flash of present gain, tho extorted from the laborer and land, to greater advantages in future."[2] These are the words of a patient as well as a

---

(1) C.O. 5/545, p. 289-290.
(2) Lans. Ms. Vol. 88, f. 157.

Van de Sande Studio, New Smyrna, Fla.
A GLIMPSE OF ONE OF THE TURNBULL CANALS, NEW SMYRNA, FLORIDA

wise director. He could not suppress this hard earned sense of gratification, because his big undertaking had brought such slow returns, that most of his friends had doubted his ultimate success and all had urged him to get his money back as quickly as possible.

With success now clearly in view, he made some important improvements which seemed to him necessary for farming in this climate. The parallel between Florida and the southern Mediterranean countries which he knew so well in former years of travel, was always before his mind, and so when a severe drought scorched his crops, he decided to institute the Egyptian method of irrigating the land,[1] which is by a closely woven net-work of canals.[2] This was entirely new to American planters and they looked on the large scale of his irrigation plan with doubtful eyes. It does indeed seem strange that in a land so plenti-

---

(1) Lans. Mss. Vol. 88, f. 157.
(2) Enc. Britannica, Vol. IX, p. 27.

fully watered, such an extensive irrigation scheme as can now be clearly traced in the canal system at New Smyrna should have been thought necessary, and visitors to the old site of New Smyrna have always thought them solely a drainage plan. But Turnbull had seen this method work marvels in the Nile country, and knew of it as a practical agricultural aid, for in 1763, just before he came to Florida, the great canal between Cairo and the Red Sea had been repaired to supply fresh water to the towns on the Suez Canal. At any rate, in this letter Turnbull expressly stated that his canals were originally for the purpose of irrigation and not of drainage,[1] though of course they accomplished the double purpose of draining the marshes and watering the high land. In a recent survey of the vicinity of New Smyrna, these canals were pronounced a fine engineering feat and designed in the best possible way to irrigate and drain that country.

---

(1) Lans. Mss. Vol. 88, f. 157.

CHAPTER VII

SPANISH INTRIGUE

THERE was no middle class in Florida at this time. Slaves were brought in shiploads direct from Africa, and some of the planters along the St. Johns River owned thousands of them. Thus the colonists at New Smyrna were an isolated class, ignored by their wealthy white neighbors as poor and small farmers, and looked upon by the negroes as "poor white trash," just as the few poor people of the Carolinas and Virginia were regarded by the slaves, all of which was naturally resented by the Minorcans. This was the feeling as well, of the indentured colonists in Georgia and Virginia, only not so pronounced, because their nationality was the same as those about them, and in a few years they could not be marked out; while the Minorcans remained a distinct class in Florida for many years. Yet, the Minorcans proved themselves vastly superior to the rest of Turnbull's colonists at New Smyrna in industry and honesty, and, while unpopular alike with Greeks, Italians and English, they kept together, and worked steadily at paying off their debt to the Company. The main complaint which they had to make against their situation, was the number of deaths which had occurred among them up to 1773, for their numbers dwindled in that time from fourteen hundred to six hundred in the nine years that they lived at New Smyrna. But aside from the natural course of events, many things happened to them which molded the opinions of succeeding generations. One of these was a plot of the Spaniards to gain a foothold in Florida once more.

For many years the political correspondence

THE NEW SMYRNA COLONY OF FLORIDA

of English governors in America had been full of the activities of France and Spain, who were trying to regain their lost provinces there. This one in the Minorcan colony was a most carefully concealed campaign, and little attention has been paid to the discovery of it, or the effect of it on these inhabitants of Florida, though the entire correspondence of the ambassadors of the King of Spain and the Catholic Bishops interested (as naive an acknowledgment as was ever recorded) has long been in print in this country. These were collected in what are known as the A. M. Brooks papers, from the records in Seville, Spain; and a translation of these documents, published under the title of "Unwritten History of St. Augustine," by Mrs. Avarette. The letters in their proper order, tell the story for themselves.

On October 20, 1769, a Spanish fishing vessel touched at the Mosquitoes on its way south to Havana and, though this was forbidden in these times of mutual suspicion and sudden warfare, Don Campos, the parish priest of the

Minorcans, managed secretly to give a letter to the Master of the vessel to be delivered to the Bishop of Cuba. The substance of the letter was that upon sailing from Minorca, Don Campos had received from the Pope authority as parish priest for three years at New Smyrna, and now that this term had expired, he wished an extension of this time for himself and Father Casanovas, the monk who had accompanied him. He also asked for Holy oil and two assistant priests for conducting divine service. The secrecy and apparent difficulty with which the letter was sent created a real stir in Catholic circles. According to subsequent letters, it seems that Don Campos was only a good, laborious priest who had been with the Minorcans three years before they sailed from home, and his secret method of communicating with his Bishop was caused by previous experience with the policy of the English Government in Minorca and Florida, of preventing correspondence between Catholic priests. But the Bishop of Cuba proceeded very cautiously to make sure that the two priests and the Minorcans were indeed Catholics, and then referred the matter to the King of Spain, so that the latter might insist upon England fulfilling her treaty promise to allow freedom of religion to her Catholic subjects, and also that Don Campos and the Minorcans might be inspired by gratitude to his Catholic Majesty for the privileges obtained for them, and be willing agents for the Spanish Government.

A secret correspondence with Havana continued for five years when, in 1774, a vessel which had lurked suspiciously near the colony, was seized by Turnbull's order, and evidence of these activities found in letters in charge of the master of the vessel. Great was the agitation of all the Minorcans! Terror seized those directly implicated, and grief the rest, because now the comforting assurances of their nearest Bishop were interrupted. A priest and several Minorcans were convicted at St. Augustine of high treason and executed, and strange fishing vessels were henceforth forbidden to touch at New Smyrna. These events definitely antagonized the Minorcans, and they continued to hear indirectly from Cuba through the few Spaniards who still remained in Florida, and who had been opposed to English rule from the first, on account of the harsh policy of Major Ogilvie, the military commander of Florida before Grant's arrival. Thus the best element of New Smyrna endured the hardships and suffered the restrictions of living in a new land under foreign masters, but joined at once the political plots of a tireless enemy of England. It is not, therefore, surprising, but nevertheless amusing, to note that the sympathetic and excitable Romans reported the seizure of the fishing vessel as 'a diabolical assault on the kindly tars for giving food to the starving Minorcans!'

A very decided change came over the affairs of administration in Florida after Moultrie's appointment as Lieutenant-Governor. In the smallest matters he showed indecision, appealed for support of his opinions to those about him and bothered Hillsborough with plaintive letters on the disobedience of his subordinates. Governor Grant had not been absent a month from Florida before Moultrie had to deal with Indian troubles at New Smyrna and his sense of insufficiency became evident.

Seventy-two Indians, led by Cowkeeper, a Creek Chief, came to New Smyrna the first part of May, under the impression that it was a settlement of Spaniards and Yemassee Indians, both bitter enemies of the Creeks. They were very sulky and, on meeting a boat's crew at Turnbull's cow pens, beat the Minorcans severely and terrified the whole community. Turnbull treated the Indians diplomatically, invited the head man to his house and gave them plenty to eat and more to drink, so that they were restored to a good humor, when he explained to them the nationality of the Minorcans, as Grant had done before, and told them that the new Governor at St. Augustine would be glad to see them. The

DR. ANDREW TURNBULL

Indians departed peaceably, though Turnbull took the precaution to send Langley Bryant and Black Sandy, a slave, to watch them until they were safely on their way.[1] Turnbull wrote to Moultrie, informing him that the Indian's attack had been a false alarm, and Moultrie reported it thus to Hillsborough. But ten days later Turnbull came to St. Augustine to confer with Moultrie, saying that he was still uneasy about the Indians and had written to his partner, Sir William Duncan, asking him to tell Hillsborough so. Moultrie was much flurried and provoked with Turnbull for not reporting this changed opinion to him before he wrote to England, and persisted in his belief that there was no danger. Elaborate explanations were hurried to England by Moultrie with a copy of Turnbull's first letter, and a reiteration by the Lieutenant Governor that there was not the slightest cause for alarm.[2] Nevertheless, Moultrie called the Council to-

(1) C.O. 5/552, pp. 28-29.
(2) C.O. 5/552, p. 91-94.

THE NEW SMYRNA COLONY OF FLORIDA

gether, and told them that since the Minorcans were disturbed, reinforcements might be sent to New Smyrna. Moultrie said the Council agreed with him that there was no danger, but that he would send a detachment of troops to the colony. It is perfectly apparent now, either there was danger and troops should have gone, or there was not and no troops should have gone! Still, Moultrie wrote to Major MacKenzie, commanding His Majesty's forces in East Florida, requesting him to send twelve men to reinforce the eight soldiers of the 31st Regiment permanently stationed there. MacKenzie's opinion of the Lieutenant Governor may be seen from the contents of his letter:

> "St. Augustine,
> June 6th, 1771.
>
> Sir:
>
> Dr. Turnbull is a Gentleman that I have the greatest regard and esteem for, and wou'd gladly wish it was in my power to quiet the Apprehensions and fears of his new Settlers by sending a reinforcement of Soldiers to the Musqueto's, as you require with the advice of his Majesty's Council. The detachment of the 31st Reg't already there is very sufficient in my humble opinion, to answer the purpose that they were sent for, that is, to prevent Mutiny and insurrection

DR. ANDREW TURNBULL

among the Greek Settlers on that Plantation. If any other Accident shou'd happen to make it seriously necessary to have more Troops sent to the Musquetos, you'll be so good as to make application to General Gage, the Commander in Chief, who no doubt will give me orders relative thereto.

I have the pleasure to be, etc.

(signed) Alec. MacKenzie."[1]

This was most cavalier treatment—it would have taken three months to get orders from General Gage for those twelve men! There ensued more complaints from Moultrie to Hillsborough, and the latter said that Moultrie was within his rights to ask for the soldiers.[2] The treatment which Moultrie received is all the more proof of his weakness when it is known that he was acting permissibly. First, he was annoyed that any report, however small, to the home government of the affair, should differ from his; then he gave his opinion that there was no danger, yet ordered the soldiers sent to New Smyrna, and was snubbed by the officer in command at St. Augustine.

---

(1) C.O. 5/552, p. 105.
(2) C.O. 5/552, p. 123.

THE NEW SMYRNA COLONY OF FLORIDA

This is but one instance of Moultrie's insecure position while in authority. He had no friends among the military men of St. Augustine, and he seemed to lack the power to make men obey him.

In the meantime, affairs in the Northern colonies had taken on such a serious aspect that the British Government wished for a stronger hand in Florida to steer her clear of the spreading discontent, for Florida people were watching the course of events with eager interest.

The Gaspin, a British revenue vessel, was burned in Narragansett Bay in 1772, and the tea ships sailed in 1773 for Charleston, Philadelphia, New York, and Boston. The colonial world held its breath in dread and expectation of their arrival, and a responsive thrill of enthusiasm ran down the coast when Boston dumped the tea into her harbor on December 16th. Now England became finally aware of the unanimous and determined attitude of her colonies, and, with kindred stubbornness, set herself to subdue them to her will.

"It was the changes, vacillation, divisions, and weaknesses of the English ministers, the utter disintegration of English parties, the rapid alterations of severity and indulgence, which had rendered all resistance to authority popular," writes one of the leading English historians of this day.[1]

A campaign of severity was in vogue from now on, and Florida had her share of it. As Turnbull, Drayton and their friends were in official disfavor since the assembly dispute, it was decided to send a man direct from England, with orders to proceed summarily to stamp out the first sign of revolutionary opinions. Colonel Tonyn, a protege of Lord Marchmont, arrived as Governor, in March, 1774; and his first act was to issue a proclamation inviting loyal Americans to come to

---

(1) Lecky, V. III, p. 403.

Florida and quit the provinces then in revolt. Florida was, by this time, the only loyal province south of Canada, and many Tories responded to his invitation, a circumstance which at once strengthened Tonyn's influence in England.

CHAPTER VIII

TURNBULL AND DRAYTON VS. TONYN AND MOULTRIE

THE outburst of anger which met the Boston Port Bill, and the calling of the First Continental Congress at Philadelphia show what strides the Revolution had made by this time. Florida and Georgia were the only colonies which were not represented at the Congress, and England took drastic measures to cut them off from the contagion. Tonyn's orders were to do something and do it quickly. It was up to him to prove to the anxious ministers that he could balk the whirlwind, and he proceeded to issue more proclamations of violent condemnation against the

DR. ANDREW TURNBULL

Revolutionists. In reality, Florida was little in sympathy with the movement because her settlers were still few and far between. Therefore, Drayton and Turnbull, with their friends, were inclined to smile at the impetuosity of the new Governor,—the Chief Justice, in particular, incurring the displeasure of the peppery colonel by his "caviling"[1] as Tonyn expressed it.

Moultrie retained his post as Lieutenant Governor, and attached himself to his new superior with ardor. He was still smarting under the slights which the officers of the garrison had dealt him, and he bore no love for Drayton and Turnbull for their part in the elections dispute, so it was natural for him to enlist the sympathies of Tonyn against them.

In November a plan of Drayton's for obtaining lands from the Indians came to light, and appeared to Tonyn a good opportunity to

---

[1] C.O. 5/555, pp. 53-60.

discipline his opponent. Jonathan Bryan, a friend of Drayton's uncle, who was then Governor of South Carolina, had offered him, two years before, a share in Apalachee Old Fields, a large tract of land on the St. Johns River which the Indians, he said, were willing to sell, because they were about to move back to the body of their nation. When Drayton had suggested going to Governor Grant with this measure, Bryan replied that the Governor was a hard bargainer in money matters and he preferred to have some one else use his influence directly in England to have the treaty ratified. Drayton told him that he had no influence there, but his friend, Dr. Turnbull, had, and that as that gentleman was about to sail for England, if Bryan wished to include the Doctor in the plan, he would ask his assistance. Bryan consented, and set about his dealings with the Indians, while Turnbull consulted his lawyers in England, who told him the affair was quite lawful.[1] A short time before his

---

(1) C.O. 5/555, pp. 277-281.

death, George Grenville had also told Turnbull to look up such a proposition and Turnbull, with his characteristic enthusiasm, urged this one along. Bryan secured the lease of the land for ninety-nine years, and left it with the Indians to show all their people; but, in 1774, at a meeting with the Governor of Georgia, this pending treaty was discovered and, as it was unknown to the authorities, Bryan, the only person named in the transaction, stood in ill favor with them.[1] Turnbull and Drayton had not yet seen the terms of the treaty or consented to be his partners—they had simply been waiting to see what he had to offer them; but when Tonyn started to prosecute Bryan for trying to make such a treaty, Drayton took up his cause. He urged that a private company had secured lands on the Ohio River in a similar fashion and been authorized to occupy them by the Government, and that since Mr. Grenville, while Prime Minister, had advised such

---

(1) C.O. 5/555, p. 281.

a course, he thought it quite permissible. There was evidently a conflict of legal opinion on this score, however, for a letter of Tonyn's to the Earl of Dartmouth refers to the latter's disapproval of such treaties.[1] That Drayton planned, nevertheless, to oppose Tonyn, is shown by the same letter. "My Lord, I am perfectly informed that Dr. Turnbull, Mr. Penman, with a few more of the Chief Justice's Creatures, are intriguing and endeavoring to raise a Faction from which I expect some hostile proceedings in our next General Sessions in December."[2] In one year, relations between Tonyn and Drayton had certainly become anything but cordial; and the General Sessions in December justified the Governor's expectations. Turnbull said that the Governor insulted the Grand Jury,[3] of which he was a member. That body drew up an address to the Honorable William Drayton, giving

---

(1) C.O. 5/556, pp. 117-118.
(2) C.O. 5/556, pp. 117-118.
(3) C.O. 5/546, pp. 53-54.

their opinion that he was entirely blameless so far as he had been concerned in the Bryan affair.[1] In addition, Drayton wrote a complete and dignified account of his letters and conversations with Bryan and presented it to the Governor. In it he said that the only reason Bryan had approached him was because he wished to get governmental sanction for his treaty and, therefore, he did not see how the matter could be viewed as an attempt to evade the law.[2] He concluded, "From the character which, I flatter myself, I have established with all that know me, for Honour and Veracity; I hope that this Representation of my every Concern in this affair, which I avow before God to be strictly true, will set my Conduct in a favorable Light, and that if it does not totally exculpate me from the imputation of having committed an Error, it will at least relieve me from the Censure of guilt."[3] Tonyn continued

---

(1) C.O. 5/556, p. 55.
(2) C.O. 5/555, pp. 277-281.
(3) C.O. 5/555, pp. 277-281.

to write to Germain, successor to Hillsborough as Secretary of the colonies, that "Dr. Turnbull and Mr. Drayton have associated with Bryan in his scandalous undertaking. That, my Lord, the blame must fall with an oppressive weight upon the Chief Justice"[1]—these extracts of letters have been given to show the impersonal manner of Drayton in contrast to the ever violent and vindictive language of Tonyn. The latter, throughout this correspondence, distinguished himself in the number of personal libels he collected to hurl at his opponents.

The early part of 1776, Tonyn suspended Drayton from his office for his championing of Bryan and wrote to England for sanction of his act.[2] St. Augustine and the plantations hummed with excitement and divided opinion. Drayton came of a prominent South Carolina family, and so the interest was by no

---

(1) C.O. 5/555, pp. 53-60.
(2) C.O. 5/556, pp. 501-502.

means local. Tonyn warned Turnbull that his name had been mentioned in the proceedings, though he had not charged him before the Board,[1] but this did not stop the angry Scotchman in defense of his friend. He felt they were in the right and he was sure of support from his friends in the home Government, so he proceeded with a strong hand. Tonyn had said that he did not believe there were six loyal subjects in the province,[1] and to disprove his assertion, Drayton's friends called a meeting of the citizens of Florida, to prepare an address of loyalty to the King, on February 27th, at Wood's Tavern. From the list of distinguished names signed to this paper, there must have been a representative gathering, though Tonyn tried to discredit it by saying that many men of no property signed their names. Turnbull parried by saying that that may have been so, "For it is not always known whether men have

---

(1) C.O. 5/155 British Transcript in Washington Library, Box 241.

THE NEW SMYRNA COLONY OF FLORIDA

Property or not, but Governor Tonyn does not mention what is well known, which is, that many of them singly have more property in the Province than the Governor and Council all put together, the Lieut. Governor excepted."[1] He ended this question sensibly by stating what was true in comparison with the other colonies—"I wish, however, for the Governor's Honor and Credit of the People that he had not said anything about Property, for that of his Province is very little indeed."[2] At any rate, there are seventy-eight names signed to this interesting Address, some of them still well known in Florida, though the majority of these people left when England gave Florida back to Spain. At the bottom, Turnbull signed his name again "on behalf of upwards of two hundred families of Greeks

---

(1) C.O. 5/546, pp. 113-115 Defense of Turnbull before Lords of Trade to Charges by Tonyn.

(2) C.O. 5/546, pp. 113-115 Defense of Turnbull before Lords of Trade to Charges by Tonyn.

DR. ANDREW TURNBULL

and other Foreigners at the Smyrna settlement."[1]

Turnbull presided at this meeting and was appointed to carry the address to England, while a committee was selected to present a copy of it to the Governor. At the conclusion

---

(1) C.O. 5/556, pp. 113-115. The Humble Address of the Inhabitants of East Florida. The full list included:

A. Turnbull	Peter Bachop	Francis Philip Fatio
Spencer Man	Joseph Michael	James Smith
Rob. Bisset	Jacobus Kip	Lewis Fatio
James Penman	Abr. Marshall	Rob. Stafford
Charles Delap	Wm. Taylor	Joseph Broomhead
Will Short	W. Woodvill	Enoch Barton
Tho. Mowbray	Alexr. Daniel	Tho. Higgins
Tho. Clark	Tho. Smart	John Cookson
Henry Hares	Donald McLean	James Moncrief
Ralph Laidler	George Lowthrup	Isaac Rwaz
George Simpson	George Rolphes	Wm. Wilson
Abraham Cooke	John Doran	Patrick Robinson
G. Mid Powell	Lewis Cuenoud	Frs. Phi. Fatio, Junr.
John Ross	James Isaac Pouly	Wm. Drayton
Jonah Mott	Samuel Reworth	James Waights
James Tims	Thomas Johnson	James Barns
John Newcomb	John Bunkley	William Sherwood
William Mills	Rob Bunkley	Alex Grant
Joseph Stout	Thomas Tustin	Charles Bernard
James Brown	Thomas Williamson	Wm. Watson
Fredk. Rolfes	Alex. Bisset	John Mason
John Tennant	Henry Sowerby	John Speir
George Grassell	Arch Lundie	A. Turnbull for upwards of two hundred Families of Greeks and other Foreigners on the Smyrna Settlement.
Wm. Johnson	Rich Sill	
James Henderson	Stephen White	
And. Turnbull, Junr.	William Reddy	

118

of business, most of the men lingered to discuss the topic of the day—Drayton's suspension—and as Turnbull had a copy of the defense of Drayton, he read it aloud, ending by asking those around him if they did not think Drayton had justified himself.[1] Another address of praise of Drayton's judicial character was the result of this talk,[2] and trouble grew apace from all these occurrences.

The next day the committee, consisting of Turnbull, Captain Bisset and other prominent men,[3] waited upon the Governor to present him with a copy of the address. "I, expecting that they were to deliver to me the original," wrote the pompous Tonyn to Germain, "fixed ten a Clock the next day for receiving it. Mr. Turnbull and six other gentlemen waited upon me and delivered the enclosed copy No. 1. Upon reading it I observed that I was well

---

(1) C.O. 5/556, p. 463, Tonyn to Turnbull.
(2) C.O. 5/556, pp. 73-77.
(3) C.O. 5/556, pp. 505-512. Extracts from Minutes of East Florida Council.

DR. ANDREW TURNBULL

pleased to see such a loyal Address; but, I was surprised that there were no names subscribed. Mr. Turnbull told me, he had the original to take home to England with him. Upon which I said "Gentlemen, I cannot conceive, that, an address presented, by a private person, can be so graciously received, as it would be through His Majesty's Representative; that I could not countenance such methods of driving things out of their proper Channel; that I considered this manner of coming to me, with a copy, without names, as an insult to me, and His Majesty's Government of this Province and, that when I received an insult, I always knew how to treat it. Having said this, I immediately retired into another Room."[1] With his letter, Tonyn sent another address to the King, with the names of all *his* friends on it! On these men and their negroes, he said, the Government could depend for assistance in case of invasion. "Your Lordship will per-

---

(1) C.O. 5/556, pp. 73-77.

THE NEW SMYRNA COLONY OF FLORIDA

ceive the contrast between these (latter) subjects and two hundred Roman Catholics fit to bear arms at the Smyrna settlement, where there has been for some time a detachment from this Garrison to keep them in order, in case of an insurrection, and for whom Mr. Turnbull in his letter to me No 5, wants further protection." This referred to the nine soldiers who had remained stationed at New Smyrna since the uprising of 1768,[1] by request from the neighboring planters.[2] Tonyn's opinion of the Minorcans was at a very low ebb at this time because they had refused to join the militia[3] which was then being raised to protect Florida from an invasion by the Revolutionists. The conclusion of this letter is an open plea for Germain's favor. "I would not trouble your Lordship with the minute

---

(1) C.O. 5/556, pp. 97-99. Turnbull's application for reinforcements against the Indians.

(2) C.O. 5/544, Grant said there should be a hundred soldiers there to protect the settlers from the Indians, and the planters from the new colonists.

(3) C.O. 5/155 British Transcript in Washington Library, Box 241.

DR. ANDREW TURNBULL

details of these matters, inconsiderable in themselves, were it not that your Lordship's humanity may lead you, my Lord, to give Mr. Drayton a hearing and perhaps Mr. Turnbull, of whose conduct I shall take notice, and that your Lordship may be guarded against misrepresentation, and falsehood and may see the necessity, of the civil officers, that are within this Province, giving their assistance to Government, instead of flying in the Face of it, which has been the case, upon every possible opportunity, by a faction here."

On March 4th, Tonyn wrote to Turnbull, and peremptorily demanded if it were true that he had discussed Mr. Drayton's case at the meeting in Wood's Tavern.[1] Turnbull answered sarcastically, "I am desired to give Information against myself, on a subject, which your Excellency seems to think culpable. If I had done anything which had a tendency that way, it would not be prudent to inform

---

(1) C.O. 5/556, p. 463, Tonyn to Turnbull.

against myself, nor could it be required of me. But as I am conscious of my own innocence, and that what I did, on the occasion you mention, was to assist a most worthy and respectable man under disagreeable Circumstances, I will relate to you, Sir, how that affair happened."[1] His account is the same as has been given, but his letter is a stinging arraignment of Tonyn. "Why am I not permitted to give my opinion in Conversation, when that opinion is founded on Conviction, and from a most intimate knowledge of Mr. Drayton in his publick and private capacities?

"If it is to gratify the Resentment which your Excellency threatened me and others with on the 28th of last Month,[2] when at your own request, a committee of seven, myself included, of the oldest and principal inhabitants of this province, waited on your Excellency in a most respectful manner to present to you a

---

(1) C.O. 5/556, pp. 89-93.
(2) When the address was presented to Tonyn.

Copy" etc.—"Reflect, Sir, that, after that publick threat, all will appear to spring from that motive—I beg leave also to remind your Excellency that I settled here under the Auspices of His present Majesty. I was even made happy by his Most Gracious wishes for my success in an undertaking never before attempted on so large a Scale by any private person, and that His Majesty was pleased to order His Governor of this Province to assist me as much as was in his power." Turnbull particularly drew blood by his slur on Tonyn's friends who were, indeed, not the most aristocratic in the community. "Weigh me, Sir, in the Balance against the Men who are your Informers, and I dare say, Sir, that you will find them men of little Property, Credit or Consequence, I cannot have any Enemies but such as come under this description—The Intentions of such Men are easily discoverable, Sir, by that Just and never failing Criterion, that all good Men endeavor to conciliate differences, but bad Men busy themselves in making and widening Breaches in Friendship and Mutual Confidence."[1]

This letter must have given the writer some artistic satisfaction for its eloquence, but it was, certainly, not a soothing message to send an official who was touchy about his dignity. The reply is a perfect blast of fury. "It is not my Intention, and it is contrary to my very nature to encroach upon the Rights of private Judgment, but I will not dispense with the power of calling the Servants of the Crown within this Province to answer and account for their Conduct when I think them blamable. * * * I plainly and fairly acquaint you, that I think your Behavior upon that occasion is of such a Nature that I intend to lay such Circumstances of it, as are come to my knowledge before the Council. I am not to be intimidated from doing what I conceive to be my duty from an apprehension that narrow-minded People may suspect me of Mean Re-

---

[1] C.O. 5/556, pp. 89-93, Turnbull to Tonyn.

sentments.—Pray, Sir, what threats do you pretend I made use of? I mentioned no Threats, I meant none—I should be sorry to be the means of any Person's ruin. I heartily sympathize with all, in disagreeable Circumstances, even when their misfortunes are premeditatedly of their own acquiring, notwithstanding frequent Reproofs and Warnings of their doing wrong indeed with no Effect. But however disagreeable it may be to me I must do my Duty." The constant source of annoyance to the ceremony-loving Tonyn comes up again in this letter. "If to this Moment I have not shown you marks of Civility and Attention it is owing to yourself, as you have not done me the favour of calling upon me, on the several Times you have been lately in Town.—I cannot omit to thank you for the favorable opinion you entertain of my Judgment in the choice I make of my Acquaintance when I am well convinced that they are of the Stamp you insinuate them to be of, I shall most certainly look out for others."[1]

---

(1) C.O. 5/556 pp. 97-100 Tonyn to Turnbull. Punctuation of the original letter is copied.

CHAPTER IX

THE FLIGHT TO ENGLAND

WILLIAM DRAYTON, since his suspension, had been visiting Turnbull, and Tonyn's reply must have caused the friends much amusement, since he had not failed to storm at every sarcastic bit in Turnbull's letter; but it struck a note of warning, for Turnbull was to be suspended, and they had no room to doubt that Tonyn's resentment would not stop there. Through many channels, other warnings came to New Smyrna, and made them realize that they must now take drastic measures to protect themselves from Tonyn's anger. Turnbull said he had "received an Information from undoubted

Authority, that Governor Tonyn intended to throw me, with some others, into the Dungeon in the Fort, where we must have perished in the hot Season from the Damp, and a total Exclusion of all circulating Air.—I was informed of this Intention by a gentleman of Truth and Honour, to whom the Governor had trusted this Secret. I have leave to mention his name if necessary; for he acquainted us all with Govr. Tonyn's Designs against us. I was also advised of it in a letter sent by Express to me. This letter is now in my Custody. This Imprisonment was intended because we had said that, in our opinion, Govr. Tonyn had suspended Mr. Drayton to gratify a private Resentment, and not for anything which he had done to deserve such a Punishment."[1] Turnbull, accordingly, planned to go to England with Drayton, secretly, before Tonyn could seize them.

In November, Tonyn had told Turnbull that

---

[1] C.O. 5/546, pp. 77-85. Turnbull before the Lords of Trade.

he had no objection to the latter's going to England, but, considering the letter in which he had said Turnbull was to be charged before the Council, as a notice that he was not to leave Florida, Tonyn did not think he would dare to sail without written permission, especially since once in a tiff over writing the leave, Turnbull had said that during Grant's time such a formality had not been necessary, but that now he wished to comply with every regulation. Another aggravation—but the Governor felt secure in having Turnbull as long as he withheld the leave.

No hint of his preparations for departure reached St. Augustine, until the morning of the day a vessel was to sail, when Tonyn heard a rumor of his intentions. He called the Captain of the vessel and asked him if this were true and the Captain replied "No, not hat he knew of, that he (Turnbull) had first aken passage, and then given it up."[1] Find-

---

) C.O. 5/556, pp. 505-512. Extracts from Minutes of Council.

DR. ANDREW TURNBULL

ing, however, that Turnbull was in town, the Governor sent the Deputy Clerk of the Council to him to say that if he intended to leave for England that day, the Governor wished to see him. Turnbull said he had been warned that this man was a spy who was to be appointed Secretary in his place, so he did not answer him pleasantly.[1] He sent word to Tonyn "That he was going to see his Son on Board, and that Mr. Penman was going with him."[2] Mr. Penman was later to suffer also for his part in this affair, but, in the meantime, Turnbull and Drayton escaped to England.

On March 30th, Tonyn held a council meeting, submitted an account of all the facts here mentioned and suspended Turnbull as Secretary of the Province and Clerk of the Council. The accusations against him were, First, publicly discussing Drayton's case, Second, Presenting only a copy of the Address to the

---

(1) C.O. 5/546, pp. 77-85.

(2) C.O. 5/556, pp. 505-512.

THE NEW SMYRNA COLONY OF FLORIDA

Governor, and Third, Leaving the Province without notice or permission. Two of the members of the Council who had voted against Drayton's suspension were absent from this meeting and Turnbull said they were probably not notified.[1] At any rate, he had one friend there who insisted at every accusation on a minority report of his objections to this suspension. This reads "Mr. Jollie observed that he had been acquainted with Mr. Turnbull for several years, and that he could not believe that Mr. Turnbull could intend to bring the Government of this Province into contempt, and that he did not think his conduct on that occasion had that tendency."[2] "Mr. Jollie is of opinion that Mr. Turnbull ought not to be suspended at this time."[3] Mr. Jollie resigned his seat in the Council and from the Bench as Assistant Judge, as a result of these proceed-

---

(1) C.O. 5/546, pp. 77-85.
(2) C.O. 5/556, pp. 505-512, Extracts from Minutes of Council. This Mr. Jollie, it will be recalled, had been prominent enough to be proposed for Grant's successors as Governor by Lord Hillsborough.
(3) C.O. 5/556, Extracts from Minutes of Council.

ings.⁽¹⁾ This was certainly the action of a brave man, as well as a loyal friend, for one does not find people who are participants in an unrighteous cause sacrificing themselves so promptly. Undoubtedly, Mr. Jollie had reason to believe that Governor Tonyn's actions would not be upheld in England. This account of Turnbull's alleged misdeeds is especially interesting, because no word of censure with regard to the management of New Smyrna is to be found there, nor any reference to the Minorcans. Tonyn had every opportunity to know of conditions at New Smyrna, for Mr. Forbes was still the visiting Minister there, and his own friend and adherent; and, if there had been anything which they, at that time, thought wrong, there is no doubt but that they would have put it down to Turnbull's discredit.

Tonyn was very anxious about what Turnbull and Drayton might say of him in England, however. He began to write Germain

---

(1) C.O. 5/546, pp. 78-85, Turnbull before Lords of Trade.

that this quarrel was not of his making, but had its roots far back in Grant's administration. "Sensible of the mean artifices and misrepresentations that these two gentlemen have made use of, to operate upon the minds of his Majesty's good Subjects of this Province; and that your Lordship may not imagine that this dissatisfaction has arisen, since I have had the honour of being Governor of this Province, or that it is well grounded, give me leave, My Lord, to mention the source from whence it has sprung.

"About the time Governor Grant left this Province, he recommended Mr. Moultrie to be appointed Lieutenant Governor.

"Mr. Turnbull expected his Friends in England would have procured him that honour.

"An enmity had subsisted between Mr. Moultrie and Mr. Drayton, Mr. Moultrie's promotion, and a considerable addition of large fortune, by the death of his father-in-law,

DR. ANDREW TURNBULL

has added envy to dislike. Mr. Turnbull's disappointment, and the malignant envy of the other, entirely corresponded, and lead them to resign their Seats in Council, and to behold every measure of internal Government in an unfavorable light." Then comes his greatest effort to discredit his enemies. "But not satisfied with that, *they carried their sympathy so far as to become Patriots for the cause of America.* It is notorious that these Servants of the Crown have reprobated the measures carried on by His Majesty's Ministers; and, that Mr. Turnbull in particular declared in Company, in a debate with Lt. Governor Moultrie, that America was in the right, the King's Ministers in the wrong, that Lord North would answer for the measures with his Head."[1] Such heresies must have made the Secretary for the Colonies smile when he remembered the thundering speeches of Burke in the sacred precincts of Parliament itself against these

---

(1) C.O. 5/556, pp. 495-498.

very measures of Government. Many loyal British subjects said openly that America was right, but did not believe she was wise to separate herself from England. But Tonyn tried to arouse Germain. "If such freedom was taken in Publick Company, where the King's Friends and Servants were present, what must have passed in their private Cabals? It is well known that the rebels have had exceedingly good information concerning the state of this Garrison, and of everything carrying on here."[1] Turnbull would have looked with amused disdain on the outburst in the final paragraph of this letter. "There are many facts which I might mention to your Lordship, that strongly mark their characters; but, none more than, the precipitate, mean secret manner that Mr. Turnbull took in leaving this Province."

On May 10th, Turnbull presented his loyal Address to Germain in London, to be delivered

---

(1) C.O. 5/556, pp. 495-498.

to the King, and asked an audience of the Secretary for the Colonies. The first result of this interview, comes out in a letter of stern reproof, from Germain to Governor Tonyn, on his treatment of William Drayton. "In times like the present it were much to be wished that all His Majesty's faithful subjects would forego every smaller consideration, and apply their Attention to the public Safety and Advantage—I will hope that your own good sense will lead you to set the Example of burying in oblivion every little Injury or Subject of Complaint, which appears to have been more the effect of Pique, or hasty Resentment, than any malevolence to your person, or settled purpose to disturb your Administration.

"In this light the Lords of Trade have considered Mr. Drayton's conduct toward you, and their Lordships have, upon a full Examination of the Charges brought against him, reported to His Majesty their opinion that his Suspension from his office of Chief Justice ought to be removed—and I am commanded

THE NEW SMYRNA COLONY OF FLORIDA

by the King to signify to you His Majesty's Pleasure that you do accordingly remove his Suspension and reinstate him in his office of Chief Justice, and that no part of his Salary be withheld on account of his suspension."[1] A curtain must be drawn on the mortification and rage of the Governor who considered his authority so precious that he was even insulted to have an address to the King through any source than his own reports. But another part of Germain's letter gave him the cue to his revenge. It read: "The very great advantage which the public must derive from the valuable Settlement at Smyrna, gives it a Claim to particular Attention; and as, in the absence of Doctor Turnbull, occurrences may arise which will require the Aid and Protection of the Government, I must recommend it to you to be very watchful to prevent any Injury or Detriment happening to the Settlement, and to give every Encouragement in

---

(1) C.O. 5/556, pp. 232-235, Germain to Tonyn.

your power to promote its Growth and the Advantage of the Proprietors"[1] Tonyn proceeded to do very queer things for the growth of New Smyrna—things which now make it a vine-choked jungle behind the cheerful little American town bearing its name.

Turnbull carried out the formality of being on leave of absence from Florida, by requesting of Germain, on July 1st, an extension of the time he had mentioned to Tonyn that he would be away. He was busy preparing a memorial for the Lords Commissioners of Trade and Plantations, wherein his charges against Governor Tonyn were fully and formally set forth.[2] Germain's letter of reproof to the Governor did not reach Florida until September, and in the meantime Tonyn showed no open hostility to the settlement. On July 19th he reported that a band of Indians had broken into some of the colonists' homes, stolen

---

(1) C.O. 5/556, pp. 232-235, Germain to Tonyn.
(2) C.O. 5/556, p. 245.

clothes and robbed the bee-hives and cornfields. Tonyn said that he called the Indians together and told them that in his country such crimes were punishable by death, but beyond warning them he took no action.[1] Turnbull received complaints from his son, that the Governor gave them no protection from these raids and that he had also prevented them being supplied with the staple foods, which they still bought by shiploads.[2] It was for this reason, Turnbull claimed, that the Minorcans refused to join the Battalion of militia which was then being raised.[3] At any rate, whether from their long-standing quarrel with England, their anti-Protestant feeling or their antipathy to the Governor, as Turnbull claimed, Tonyn said, "I fear by what Colonel Bisset mentions, we cannot venture to raise at Doctor Turnbull's Settlement more than one Company."[4] The

---

(1) C.O. 5/568, Tonyn to Germain, pp. 337-338.
(2) C.O. 5/155, British Transcripts in Congressional Library at Washington, D. C., 241.
(3) C.O. 5/155 British Transcripts, Congressional Library, Box 241.
(4) C.O. 5/556, p. 744, Tonyn to Germain.

DR. ANDREW TURNBULL

probabilities are that the long absence of Turnbull, and the hostility of the Governor, had precipitated many troubles. Andrew Turnbull, Jr., his nephew, was not able to control his overseers, who were, undoubtedly, brutal to the people. These farmers had come from an island where there was no great aristocracy to oppress them, and they were independent and often impertinent by their own reports,[1] but their punishments must have been out of all proportion to their offenses. Whenever they complained to young Andrew Turnbull, they had to speak through their interpreters, the very men who oppressed them.[2] The lash and irons, so frequently and cruelly used in England and the other colonies,—Virginia, for example—were new to them, and their hatred of their oppressors grew daily. Indian depredations and trouble with food shipments completed their disgust. So when the news of the successful invasion of Florida by the new

---

(1) C.O. 5/557.
(2) C.O. 5/557 pp. 439-440.

THE NEW SMYRNA COLONY OF FLORIDA

American Government, hostile to England, reached them, they began to hope that their deliverance was at hand. Andrew Turnbull, Jr., wrote on September 1st, when an American Privateer appeared on the coast, "I cannot say what might be the consequence regarding the white people, as there is a good number of them at present a little discontented, and I am fully persuaded would join the Rebels immediately on their landing at Smyrna."[1] He knew by experience that it was useless to apply directly to Governor Tonyn for help, but wrote to Mr. Gordon and Colonel Bisset, who wrote to Tonyn that "This Information is very alarming, especially with regard to Dr. Turnbull's people, a great number of whom would certainly join them—those that joined them of the Smyrna Settlements, would endeavor to plunder our plantations—I shall set out immediately for Smyrna and will make the best disposition I can for the defense of the Place by

---

(1) C.O. 5/556, p. 767, Andrew Turnbull to Arthur Gordon, Esq.

arming those we can trust and disarming the suspected."[1]

Then came the letter reinstating Drayton, and the fate of New Smyrna was sealed. Tonyn wrote to Germain, "I have always been active to promote the prosperity of it (New Smyrna) although I have ever doubted of its success. Such, My Lord, has been the state of that Settlement from its Commencement, that it has been always necessary to post a military guard there, to prevent trouble and insurrection"—(those eight soldiers who acted as policemen for that whole section of the country)—"and I am sorry to acquaint your Lordship, that at this Critical Juncture, it is a thorn in our side, as I am just now obliged to reinforce that Guard to preserve internal good order, when the Troops are much wanted to oppose the depredations of the Rebels on our north frontiers."[2]

---

(1) C.O. 5/556, pp. 771-772, Bisset to Tonyn.
(2) C.O. 5/556 p. 765.

THE NEW SMYRNA COLONY OF FLORIDA

Meanwhile, Turnbull thought he was settling all his troubles in England. On September 19th,[1] and December 6th[2] he presented two Memorials before the Lords of Trade. The gist of both is the same, except that one is fuller of detail in some charges, one in others. When the first Memorial was presented, Lord Marchmont (Tonyn's sponsor) appeared before the Lords of Trade and had the charges set aside on the grounds that they included crimes other than so-called State Crimes and so did not come under the business of that body. Therefore, Turnbull prepared the second Memorial, confining himself to Tonyn's State Crimes.[3] They include the most serious accusations—everything, in fact, except disloyalty to England. He commenced by saying that Tonyn had refused "to grant lands to many Persons who had Titles to claim the same, particularly to your Memorialist, to

---

(1) C.O. 5/546, pp. 49-51.
(2) C.O. 5/546, pp. 53-54.
(3) Lansdowne Mss. Vol. 66, pp. 725-727.

DR. ANDREW TURNBULL

William Drayton, James Penman, Donald Maclean and others. And the said Governor has taken upon himself to grant Lands to such as had no claim nor Right thereto, namely to Alexander Gray, Alexander Skinner, James Forbes and others, which may be proved by the Records in the Secretary's Office."[1] Second, that he had "Taken it upon him, to decide Causes cognisable in the Courts of Justice only, and also of examining into private contracts and agreements, particularly in calling for, and examining into the Validity of the Deeds of Agreement between your Memorialist and the People of the Smyrnia Settlement"[2] "Which created such a Diffidence and Apprehension of the Validity of these Deeds of Agreement as disturbed the Peace, Order and Industry of the Smyrnia Settlement so much that its Ruin and Loss of that great Property was with Difficulty prevented by

---

(1) C.O. 5/546, pp. 49-51.
(2) C.O. 5/546, pp. 49-51.   Smyrna spelled "Smyrnia" in these documents.

your Memorialist."[1] So, evidently the contracts had been investigated before Turnbull left for England, and had been found valid, for no settlers left New Smyrna until two years after this. But the alarm of the Minorcans here referred to was due to a doubt which Tonyn circulated as to their right to own lands in Florida under the grant which Turnbull held. The old clause requiring that the settlers be Protestants was unearthed and challenged, and the Minorcans were told that Turnbull intended to cheat them of their allotted land when their term of servitude had expired. It required little effort to spread the inference that since this could be done, it had been planned by Turnbull from the beginning. It was with difficulty that he had explained that by the same clause he could have deprived them three years after they had settled. And the damning fact remained that *somebody* actually could deprive them of their hard-earned land

---

(1) C.O. 5/546, pp. 53-54.

DR. ANDREW TURNBULL

by officially revealing their religion and producing Turnbull's grant. It mattered little to them that England and not Turnbull was responsible for this policy—they hated England and longed for Spanish rule to bring again their familiar language and the Catholic religion to Florida. Their confidence in Turnbull was destroyed and his name became an anathema to them. This was the situation which Turnbull left behind him in Florida though he did not know that Tonyn would be bold enough to deliberately push on the ruin of New Smyrna in the face of ministerial disapproval. Tonyn was indeed unprincipled in all his methods, for the Memorials continued to say that he had borrowed money from many people in Florida, giving them in exchange, bills payable by men in London, and these men had declared "they had none of Tonyn's money in their hands" so the bills were protested and returned to America through the hands of Mr. John Graham of Georgia and Mr. James Penman of Florida. Turnbull flatly

THE NEW SMYRNA COLONY OF FLORIDA

called this swindling, and declared with withering sarcasm that as it had not been tried before in Florida, it must be termed one of Governor Tonyn's innovations![1] In addition to this practice, Tonyn had contrived to get Receipts for public work done and then refused to pay the carpenters and other workmen, so that the chief master builder refused to repair the platform for the guns in Fort George on this account.[2] Tonyn had also bought up staple provisions and put them in the hands of a monopoly to be sold at double price.[3] An accusation against Tonyn which followed this is particularly interesting because a year later Tonyn made the same charges against Turnbull. Turnbull said "That Govr. Tonyn's Cruelties to his Servants and Negroes which he often inflicts with his own Hands, (for he generally is the Executioner himself), is an intolerable Nuisance, and greatly distressing

---

(1) C.O. 5/546, pp. 49-51, 4th Charge.
(2) C.O. 5/54, pp. 49-51, 5th Charge.
(3) C.O. 5/546, pp. 49-51, 6th Charge.

DR. ANDREW TURNBULL

to the Inhabitants of St. Augustine; not only by the Cries of the Sufferers, and a total disregard of all Decency in the Mode of his Punishments, but also by the Severity of them, which he carries to an incredible Height of Inhumanity, and by Cruelties unheard of before in that Province."[1] Turnbull claimed that Drayton had been suspended two days before the trial of Tonyn's coachman for flogging a man to death, because Drayton would have found out that Tonyn was present and party to that crime.[2] What irony of fate it is to know that the writer of these words has, through Tonyn's friends, borne a more terrible name for cruelty than even his shocked description of the Governor's actions portrayed! Finally, by suspending Chief Justice Drayton, and Turnbull, and by accusing the last Grand Jury of being "Drayton's Creatures," he had acted from personal rancor rather than a sense of justice. "Govr. Tonyn's

---
(1) C.O. 5/546, pp. 49-51, 6th Charge.
(2) Lansdowne Mss. Vol. 88, ff 173-174.

conduct on the whole has been such as has entirely lost him the Confidence of the People. Your Memorialist therefore prays That, for the Honour and Advantage of His Majesty's Service, and for restoring the Peace and Tranquillity of the Province of East Florida, Govr. Tonyn be removed from that Government."[1] Certainly this is a black record, but north of Florida there were thousands of Revolutionists engaged in depriving England herself of an empire, and their crimes seemed to the Lords of Trade more serious than the misdeeds of Tonyn against individuals. Moreover, here was a governor who had stuck to his post when every other Royal governor had been driven from the colonies. Turnbull could not say Tonyn had any sympathy for America's cause—far from it—he had sent Indians, privateers, proclamations, a small reign of terror by land and sea, against the colonials. Therefore, Germain, who pre-

---

[1] C.O. 5/546, p. 51, Conclusion of Memorial.

DR. ANDREW TURNBULL

sided at these meetings of the Lords of Trade, advised Turnbull not to insist on his complaints being heard at that time, alleging that "It would be a tedious and troublesome Business to Administration, who then had Affairs of great National Importance on their Hands." "You also, engaged, My Lord," wrote Turnbull, recalling this audience, "that Govr. Tonyn would be more cautious in future, which I then doubted, but was answered by your Lordship, that there were such Promises and Vouchers for him, that he would certainly behave better than before."[1] And so, Tonyn did not lose his office, but received another reproof from Germain,[2] and an order, from the Lords of Trade, to "Lose no time in preparing such proofs and depositions as he may think necessary for his own defense, and to give full license for the same purpose to all persons on

---

(1) Turnbull to Germain British Transcripts, Box 41, Lansdowne Ms. Vol. 1219, fo. 40.

(2) C.O. 5/556, pp. 695-697. Germain said to Tonyn that his actions were Conduct in a Governor that appears to be rather the effect of sudden passion than Moderation and sound Policy."

behalf of the Memorialists."[1] Turnbull waited in London and made his defense before the Lords of Trade to that list of charges for which Tonyn had suspended him on March 30, 1776. As Drayton had already been exonerated from his part in the Bryan affair, and as Turnbull's part was even less than his, it is not necessary to relate his answer to this part of the charge. The next was that Turnbull had made use of his faction to have himself appointed, instead of the Governor, to present a "Loyal Address" to the King. Turnbull denied this, and said that the Agent of the Province had first been considered, instead of the Governor, the latter of whom "The voters objected to, as he had shown himself adverse and hostile to the meeting of the Inhabitants, suspecting that it was intended to draw up Complaints against him."[2] The last charge, Turnbull's leaving the Province without written permit had already been dismissed by Ger-

---

(1) C.O. 391/88, p. 200. Extract from Journal of Trade and Plantations.
(2) C.O. 5/546, pp. 77-85. Defense of Turnbull before Lords of Trade.

DR. ANDREW TURNBULL

main who himself granted Turnbull an extension of leave.

Turnbull's business in England was concluded by April 14, 1777, when Germain wrote the result of the investigations to Governor Tonyn. It is a statesman-like document, and worthy to be quoted for its handling of the whole question.

"Whitehall
14th April 1777.

Governor Tonyn
Sir,

In my Letter to you of the 2d Instant, I avoided taking notice of your Suspension of Dr. Turnbull from his Office of Secretary, and of the Instances you State of his Misbehavior which induced you to take that Step; for as he had also exhibited a Complaint against you, to the Board of Trade, it necessarily became my Duty to lay the whole Matter before their Lordships, and until they should make their Report to His Majesty, no Opinion could be formed of the propriety of your Conduct.

A Discussion of this nature, especially where the Parties have many & powerful Friends who, on account of their great Property in Florida will naturally interest themselves in the Decision, soon becomes a more serious Business than the original Matter seemed to promise; and in this Case, whatever the final Determination might have been, the Consequences of the Proceed-

THE NEW SMYRNA COLONY OF FLORIDA

ing must unavoidably have proved disagreeable to you.

The Common Rules of Justice would have required that you should have been heard in support of your Charge against Dr. Turnbull, as well as in your Defense against the Accusations brought by him against you, and I could not have advised the King to permit you to leave the Province of East Florida at such a Crisis without sending out a Person to succeed you in the Governm't on whose Ability and Zeal for His Majesty's Service I could have the same Reliance as I have upon yours. To avoid the Necessity of so disagreeable a Step, I thought it best to endeavor to get rid of the whole Matter, and which I was the more desirous of doing, as from what I had seen of it, there did not appear to be any sufficient Ground for a serious Inquiry. I took, therefore, some Pains to convince Dr. Turnbull that it was greatly (to) his Interest, and that of his Connexions, as a Planter, as well as his Duty as a Servant of the Crown to live upon good Terms with the Governor of the Province; that where nothing of Injustice or Violence could be alleged to have happened, offences proceeding from mere Mistakes, or Infirmities that were perhaps constitutional, should be passed over among Men engaged in the common Cause of supporting the Rights of the Crown & promoting the Prosperity of the Province; That, on your part, I had no doubt he would find a Disposition to bury in Oblivion every past Offence & to show him that Civility & Attention which his great Share in the public Stake so well entitled him to, and that if he conducted himself with the same Propriety towards you, mutual confidence and Friendship must be the happy effect, an Event which must greatly serve to promote the public prosperity, by restoring Harmony among the principal people of the Province. Finding what I had said made all the

DR. ANDREW TURNBULL

Impression I could wish, & perceiving him thoroughly disposed to adopt the Mode of Conduct I had recommended, I proposed to him, that he should take the first Step towards a Reconciliation, and withdraw his complaint against you; That I would then withhold from the Lords of Trade all Cognizance of your Charges against him, and recommend to you to remove his Suspension, upon Condition of his making a suitable Acknowledgment of the Impropriety of his Conduct in quitting the Province without your Leave in Writing, & giving Assurance of a candid & respectful Behavior towards you in future. This proposal he very readily embraced, and as I cannot doubt his Sincerity, it now only remains with you to accept of the Conditions, and to put an End to an Altercation which must, in the present Circumstances of Affairs be very injurious to the King's Service, and highly detrimental to the Province. To afford a proper Opportunity for so desirable an Issue, I make Dr. Turnbull the Bearer of this Letter; and I shall extend it no further than to add my sincere Wishes that it may be the Occasion of restoring that good Humour & mutual Confidence among the King's Officers, which is at all times necessary, but at present is so essential to the public Safety and Advantage.

I am &c.

Geo. Germain."[1]

---

(1) C.O. 5/557, pp. 115-121.

CHAPTER X

THE FALL OF NEW SMYRNA

TONYN had known, since Drayton's reinstatement, which way the wind blew; and he had been proceeding industriously to execute justice upon his enemies himself. Tempting offers were made to the Minorcans to join the Militia, freedom from indentures, land in St. Augustine, assurances of protection if they ran away—all were put before them by Mr. Forbes' agents, most conspicuous of whom was Joseph Purcell, the Minorcan interpreter, who later went to work as draughtsman for Romans.

The latter part of March, a few of the settlers came to St. Augustine. The manner of their escape from New Smyrna is picturesquely told by Romans. On the pretense of making a fishing trip to the coast, (Romans must have forgotten that he had said previously the Minorcans were forbidden to fish) a small group of men received leave of absence for several days, and, on reaching the beach, at once set out to walk the eighty miles north to St. Augustine. They were hardy countrymen now, and knew their ground, so they reached St. Augustine safely, and swam Matanzas Inlet with their clothes on their heads. Tonyn simply told Germain that they were persuaded to return, but they must have received some assurances of support for, the 1st of May, ninety men appeared in town, demanding to be released from their indentures, which they declared had expired. They applied to the District Attorney, Mr. Henry Yonge, Jr., who told them they must make their complaints before a Justice of the Peace, which they accordingly did. Eighteen men were chosen to represent the rest who were told by Governor Tonyn to return and secure the crops.[1] Mr. Yonge formally reported these occurrences to the Governor and said: "I observe a number of Cruelties and indeed Murders committed by some of the Doctor's servants (which from his character certainly could never had come to his knowledge). I therefore think it my duty to lay a Copy of the Several Depositions before your Excellency."[2] How he could have read the depositions, as sworn to by the Minorcans, and thought that Turnbull was ignorant of them is inconceivable. Either his statement is a studied pose, or he did not believe all the accusations made in these documents, for many of them were astonishing charges against Turnbull himself.

Upon first reading these short but dreadful papers, the writer was inclined to try to revise the point of view of this narrative and to show

---

(1) C.O. 5/557, pp. 420-422.
(2) C.O. 5/557, pp. 225-226.

DR. ANDREW TURNBULL

Turnbull as the villain he was painted, but the whole preceding correspondence, mass of documents and public papers were in direct conflict with such a viewpoint and clearly showed such a position historically wrong—they bore nothing but testimonials in Turnbull's favor. Then, on re-reading the Minorcans' statements, and thoroughly analyzing them, a harmonizing solution offered itself, for it was found that all the charges of violent crime were placed against Turnbull's overseers, without implicating Turnbull himself. The misdeeds with which he was personally credited, were fraudulent dealings with his settlers, or small meannesses worthy only of an irresponsible or ignorant underling or servant. The most serious charges made against Turnbull were that he refused to allow the men to leave when their indentured time was up, and even forced two witnesses to sign a forged contract against Lewis Sanche in order to prolong his term.[1]

---

(1) C.O. 5/557, pp. 479-480. All of these charges are to be found in C.O. 5/551, and several page references being given here simply to locate a few specific charges.

Sanche was an overseer, but one who was in favor with those of the colony who made complaints. He said that Turnbull had ordered him to beat the people very hard and not to mind killing a man, but that he had refused. Beyond a doubt, if these charges were true, Turnbull was not the good man that he had always been considered, but the hitherto unknown events leading up to these affidavits have been related in much detail because they do not by any means bear out these statements. Turnbull was the friend and partner of a Prime Minister and a Member of the British Cabinet, he was well known to have other powerful friends[1] and to have been the social protege of that estimable man, the Earl of Shelburne.[2] The lifelong friendship of such men as William Drayton, James Penman and Captain Bisset is testimonial enough that he could not have been such a petty schemer and monster of

---

(1) C.O. 5/557, pp. 115-121, Germain to Tonyn.

(2) British Transcripts, Box 41, Cong. Library, Lansdowne Mss. 1219, fo. 34.

cruelty as these accusations describe. When it is considered that his reputation rests upon the statement of a Governor who had been for two years his outspoken enemy for other reasons, and the accusations of a few of the poor foreigners, whom no one could blame for wishing to escape servitude, it must be left to the impartial judge to declare whether their stories of Turnbull are true or not. There is no reason to believe that during the latter period of the colony, the Minorcans at times were not ill-treated by the overseers, however. Their stories of the ingenious cruelties of some of their overseers are too fully and heartrendingly told to be denied. They are the voices of the innumerable difficulties of the colony now reaching a climax. The undertaking was too large for a private concern and yet the English government was unwilling to shoulder it in such turbulent times, while the Governor was a political enemy of the proprietor, and reluctant to guard against Indian raids or to urge merchants to deliver shipments of supplies in the face of Revoluntionary disturbances. Add to this the religious pressure brought to bear by Spain on the colonists and their natural distaste for a long term of service in a community of freeholders and it is easy to see how men without proper authority or scruples could lead the Minorcans to believe that the future held nothing for them at New Smyrna.

Between May and July, 1777, Tonyn said that many of the settlers were freed by the Courts and the rest set at liberty by Turnbull's attorneys.[1] As a matter of fact, the only ones freed by the Courts were a few who had been contracted for by their parents when under age. The Court of Sessions declared the others still legally bound to serve the proprietors of New Smyrna and ordered them back to the settlement.[2] But Governor Tonyn had by this time firmly implanted in their minds the

---
(1) C.O. 5/557, No. 42.
(2) Sackville Mss. America, 1755-7, No. 100, also Lans. Mss. Vol. 66, pp. 725-727.

DR. ANDREW TURNBULL

idea that he would protect them if they repudiated their contracts. When they were confined to prison and a diet of bread and water until they should consent to fulfill their contracts, Tonyn sent them extra provisions and forced Mr. Penman, Turnbull's attorney, to pay for these things.[1] Encouraged by the Governor's disregard of the Courts, the whole settlement moved bag and baggage to St. Augustine, despite the protests of Turnbull's attorneys. But no provision whatever had been made for housing or feeding these people, and sixty-five of them died (without medical attendance being offered them) after sleeping under the trees and beside old walls in the heavy rains of August and September.[2] There had not been a single death at New Smyrna during the ten months of Turnbull's absence in England, but there were ten deaths a week among these unfortunates after they came to St.

---

(1) Lansdowne Mss. Vol. 66, pp. 725-727.
(2) Sackville Mss. America, 1755-7, No. 100.

Augustine. In December over a hundred women and children were begging around the Governor's house for bread. The men who were still able bodied had taken service on the cruisers or enlisted in the corps of Rangers, and the remainder were left to build miserable hovels for the women and children on the small lots assigned to them north of St. Augustine. They had no money with which to buy supplies to start farming and led a most precarious existence as fishermen along the shore of the Inlet. Tonyn was not seriously concerned about them—they had served his purpose and were left to shift for themselves.

Since Turnbull could not say that Tonyn was disloyal, he did not succeed in having him removed from office, but he returned to America triumphantly bearing his own reinstatement in office.[1] When he landed in New York in November, 1777, he received his first news of the ruin of New Smyrna and an

---

(1) C.O. 5/557, pp. 115-121.

DR. ANDREW TURNBULL

embargo on ships held him there in a state of great uncertainty and distress for some time. Needless to say, his relations with the Governor were anything but cordial when he finally reached Florida. He found his colonists settled in St. Augustine, without provisions, his property damaged by American raiders and Indians, and crops in the worst condition they had been in since the beginning of the colony. He openly accused Tonyn of being the cause of this wholesale destruction. Some idea of the value of the larger part of the equipment at New Smyrna and of the extent of this loss is given in the account of carpentry work completed by 1777:[1]

	Pounds
Dr. Turnbull's house	270
2 Large store houses	500
1 Smaller store house	100

---

(1) Treasury, 77/7.

Wind mill	300
Indigo house	100
145 Other houses @ 35 pounds each	5075
4 Bridges, cedar, @ 30 pounds each	120
22 Double sets of Indigo vats	1100
	7565

or $37,390.01¼

One of Tonyn's methods of working among the Minorcans is revealed in a short battle of words over the aforementioned Joseph Purcell, one of Tonyn's interpreters. Turnbull accused Purcell of serving the ends of his enemies and stirring up revolt at New Smyrna; and Purcell wrote to the Governor to be exonerated, receiving in reply a letter of praise for his upright character and a broadside of condemnation for Turnbull. "You are at liberty to make use of this Letter in your Justification against the Calumnies of the Malicious," concluded the Governor. Turnbull must have, also, accused Purcell of exaggerating the charges of the colonists, for

DR. ANDREW TURNBULL

Tonyn says, in the same letter, "I had no reason to think that in the presence of so many Witnesses, that you did not explain that Language into English without exaggeration."[1]

Tonyn's description to Germain of his coup de grace at New Smyrna is not without grim humor. "In obedience to your Lordship's commands, I have paid, My Lord, and shall pay, particular attention to the Smyrna Settlement; but, my Lord, I am convinced that your Lordship does not desire that I should give the least countenance to Injustice, Tyranny and Oppression."[2] He took occasion to complain that Drayton refused to have the Minorcans' case brought before him, directing another Magistrate to preside. Drayton was always careful to avoid the appearance of partizanship while in office. The judge who took his place instructed the colonists to return

---

(1) C.O. 5/558, pp. 499-500. Letters from Tonyn to Purcell, May 27, 1778.
(2) C.O. 5/557, pp. 420-422.

THE NEW SMYRNA COLONY OF FLORIDA

to New Smyrna and finish their contracts with Turnbull, a decision which would certainly have been challenged as colored by friendship for Turnbull if it had been rendered by Drayton. Tonyn calmly announced the most evident falsehood concerning the financial consequences of his actions at New Smyrna: "Whatever Ideas the gentlemen in England concerned in it (New Smyrna) have of its success, I will venture My Lord, to affirm, and I am confident that the discharging of the white people will be no real loss to them; as the expense of their and their Families' maintenance will ever equal the value of their labor."[1] Germain's opinion of his high handed course may be gathered from his reply to Tonyn.

"Whitehall
19th Feby. 1778

Govr. Tonyn
Sir
* * *

The desertion of the Smyrna Settlement by the People is an unfortunate circumstance for the province and must occasion a severe loss to the Proprietors. If it be in your power to lessen that loss, or to give them

---

(1) C.O. 5/557, pp. 420-422.

DR. ANDREW TURNBULL

any assistance in retrieving their Affairs, I must desire you will exert your Endeavors on their behalf.

I am, etc.,

Geo. Germain."[1]

No comment on the black charges heaped against Turnbull is to be found. Tonyn had spent his thunder in England in vain, but he had accomplished his destructive purposes in Florida without official sanction. Turnbull found that the young men of the colony had been sent to help the Indians scalp the American settlers on the Georgia border, a mission which Tonyn declared was favored by England. "If this is the case, I cannot expect any redress," wrote Turnbull in great indignation at this cruelty to defenseless women and children, but he added, "If the Grenvilles join me, I am resolved to pursue this Governor of an American Province to infamy."[2] Messrs. Penman, Drayton and Bisset declared that Tonyn deliberately broke up the settlement to

---

(1) C.O. 5/558, p. 487.
(2) Lans. Mss. Vol. 88, f. 113.

get recruits for his Rangers, since there were more men of fighting age in the colony than in the rest of the Province.[1]

On August 7, 1778, Turnbull wrote a curt note to Tonyn, saying that he intended to live in St. Augustine henceforth, and would act himself as Secretary and Clerk of the Council.[2] Tonyn stood his ground—he replied that he could enjoy the salary, but that his conduct, since his return from England, had been so extraordinary that he would not allow him the exercise of his offices.[3] This conduct was admitted and described by Turnbull himself: "The misery and wretchedness in which I found the Smyrnean people provoked me to reproach Governor Tonyn with it in such a tone and terms as I never made use of before to any Gentleman; which contrary to his usual man-

---

(1) Lans. Mss. Vol. 66, pp. 725-727.
(2) C.O. 5/558, p. 487.
(3) C.O. 5/558, p. 491.

DR. ANDREW TURNBULL

ner, he took very tamely."[1] But Tonyn sent some one else to do his fighting for him. "A few days ago," wrote Turnbull, "he sent a big man of his connections to insult me, but he proved so much of a bully that he put up with the reproof of a good cane for his Impertinence." The old Scotchman was not to be tamed, and so Tonyn retaliated by depriving him of his Secretaryship. Though he continued to fight gamely, his ruin and the failure of his long cherished settlement weighed heavily upon Turnbull. "I do not give Tonyn or his mean Prowler Lieut. Gov. Moultrie, the Satisfaction of seeing that their underhand Machinations or avowed oppressions affect me in the least."[2] It was the harshness with which his family was treated in his absence which had wounded Turnbull most of all. Mrs. Turnbull had been kept in a constant state of terror by the governor who refused to send protection to the settlement, but sent such threats,

---

(1) Lans. Mss. Vol. 88, f. 173-4.
(2) Lans. Mss. Vol. 88 f. 193.

rumors and warnings to induce her to leave her post at New Smyrna, that she kept a small vessel ready to fly at a moment's notice, to the Bahamas. Her health and spirits were for a time seriously impaired, and Turnbull vowed that "The treatment of my family in my absence can never be forgiven."[1] I really believe," he said in the tone of fond protection which he always used when alluding to his wife, "that he is the only Person, male or female, she ever knew that would have given her such Pain, especially when without a Protector."[2]

A letter to Germain from Tonyn again begs for Turnbull's dismissal, but on the ground of disloyalty to England, very probably because of the latter's outspoken disapproval of the scalping raid into Georgia. Tonyn makes an interesting admission about the Revolution in

---

(1) Lans. Mss. Vol. 88 ff. 175-6.
(2) Lans. Mss. Vol. 66, p. 714.

DR. ANDREW TURNBULL

this letter.[1] "They (Turnbull and his friends) are gentlemen, but, my Lord, in all the colonies, Georgia excepted, the principal people have been at the head of this rebellion."[2] This must have been a very reluctant admission on Tonyn's part, for Turnbull's disdain had dug deep into his official pride. Twice he mentioned in letters the fact that, for two years, when Turnbull came to town, he had not paid his respects at the Governor's house, but passed by with his friends in haughty aloofness. The fact that the higher officers at the post in St. Augustine still sided with Turnbull was a similar thorn in the Governor's side, for not only did they treat him cavalierly, but their absence deprived his court of their social prestige. Tonyn accused General Prevost and Lieut. Colonel Fuser of disloyalty and affection for Turnbull's cause, adding to this list Mr. Penman and Mr. Mann.[3] The longer

---

(1) C.O. 5/558, pp. 101 fo. 3-4.
(2) C.O. 5/558, pp. 101-103-104.
(3) Historical Mss. Commission. Amer. Mss. in Royal Institution V. 11, pp. 127-8; Letter from Tonyn to Gen. S. Henry Clinton.

the Governor's list of "traitors" grew, the more creditable they appeared—the soldiers and planters who had made Florida prosperous under Governor Grant.

Both of Turnbull's partners had died, and the period for division of their grants had passed, so their heirs in England, seeing that the colonists were disbanded, now requested a division of the grants according to their agreement. Tonyn, of course, received this information officially, and though Turnbull protested that he was quite willing to divide and had filed his papers and accounts with the Attorney General, the management of the property was taken over by Tonyn. The latter said that Turnbull's conduct during these proceedings was extravagant, and it may well be imagined that the hot-headed old Scotchman, long an autocrat in Florida, fought at bay like a wounded tiger. His family was living in St. Augustine, now, his younger sons at school, his grown son and daughters joining the faction which was rocking the tiny capital with its quarrel. In one of his complaints against this friction, an interesting hint of the extent of his former travels comes out, "It is extraordinary that a man who lived long in Turkey, who wandered among wild Arabs and was even respected in Barbary, cannot live under the English Governor of an American province."[1] The Minorcans, who lived in the section of the city assigned to them by Tonyn, did not detract from the bitterness of the feeling on both sides, and their former condition of indenture was represented to them by the champions of the Governor as degrading and cruel. It was, verily, a tempest in a teapot. On June 24, 1778, when about one thousand Americans landed at Amelia Narrows, and started to cut a passage through, there was such dissension between the officers and their men that Colonel Fuser could not muster enough men to oppose the invaders, and had

---

(1) Lans. Mss. Vol. 88, ff. 173-174.

to retire and fortify St. Johns Bluff, near the mouth of the St. Johns River.[1] On August 30th of the same year, the Americans sailed down the coast and carried off thirty negroes from New Smyrna,[2] but soon after this, the brilliant campaign of General Prevost in Georgia, removed the press of the Revolution beyond the Florida boundary.

---

(1) Forbes, p. 29.
(2) C.O. 5/569, p. 79.

CHAPTER XI

THE FIGHT FOR THE PROPERTY

THE suit against Turnbull for division of the New Smyrna property occupied the whole of the year 1779, during which time the estate was in the hands of Moultrie and Tonyn, attorneys for the English partners.[1] It scandalized Turnbull, an ardent student of legal precedent, for Tonyn to act as attorney for his partners, judge in the suit and accuser against him. His letters to Lords Shelburne and Germain fairly bristle with wrath and outraged justice. By this time, however, things had gone so badly

---

(1) Lansdowne Mss. V. 1219, fo. 34.

DR. ANDREW TURNBULL

with the English cause in America that the harassed ministers paid no attention to him. Things were going very badly for his party in Florida too. Drayton had finally been removed for his refusal to allow the Minorcans' cases to be tried in his court, and was living at Magnolia Gardens, then known as Drayton House, near Charleston. As a final insult, Tonyn declared that he believed Turnbull intended to join Mr. Drayton in Charleston and evade paying an indebtedness charged to him on the Smyrna estate. This was all the more absurd, since Tonyn himself had said that Turnbull's reverses had left him without money, so he had nothing with which to pay anyway.[1] Then an order requiring him to pay four thousand pounds bail was issued against him on February 17, 1780, and on his failure to give it, he was placed in the custody of the Provost Marshal. Turnbull filed his demurrer to this action, in which he declared

---

(1) C.O. 5/558, pp. 484-6, Tonyn to Wm. Knox.

THE NEW SMYRNA COLONY OF FLORIDA

that, for his own sake, he had no intention of leaving Florida until the estate was divided, and that he had furnished every document and account in his possession to hasten the settlement.[1]

As a matter of fact, Tonyn was using Germain's request, already quoted, that he aid the partners in England in recovering their property, to ruin Turnbull. Tonyn did not at this time even know the names of the heirs of Turnbull's partners and issued his orders against Turnbull, using the name of Earl Temple, who had died previously.

Turnbull did indeed plan to leave Florida as soon as New Smyrna was divided, for he wrote to his old friend the Earl of Shelburne for a letter of introduction to Lord Cornwallis at Charleston.[2] He was still in the custody of the Provost Marshal and the illegality of

---

(1) British Transcripts, Box 41, folio 49, Lans. Mss. Library of Congress.
(2) British Transcripts, Box 4, in Congressional Library at Washington. Lans. Mss. 1219, fo. 34.

the measures which had been taken against him by Tonyn was clear and bitter in his mind. His family alone was his consolation. "Mrs. Turnbull presents her Respects to your Lordship. We are happy in seeing that the part of our family which is formed turn out well, two out of three Daughters are married much to our Mind, and the third is promised. My eldest Son, after having had as liberal an Education as I could give him, has most cheerfully taken to farming as an Employment, and for a better Reason, that is, to get a living by it. My three youngest sons are at School here, and promise well. This Detail, my Lord, would be impertinent and troublesome to many, but I am not apprehensive that it will be so to your Lordship."[1]

Two days after this Turnbull wrote another long and masterly account of Tonyn's actions, to Germain, with the advice of his attorney on

---

(1) Lansdowne, Vol. 1219, fo. 34, British Transcripts, Box 41, Congressional Library, Washington.

the many points of law which Tonyn had overridden, but the heirs of his partners, entirely in Tonyn's hands, refused to arbitrate or settle the estate except by a suit in Chancery which Turnbull could not now afford.[1]

Finally through the combined pleas of his attorney, Mr. Penman and his friends in England, he arrived at an understanding with Lady Mary Duncan and the Grenvilles, the heirs of his original partners. Though they owed Turnbull for late disbursements, and though he had secured by his efforts more additional grants of land than they, only a small part of the estate remained for Turnbull.[2] He was not allowed his liberty under any other condition than the surrender of all but a small portion of his share.[3] He accordingly relinquished claim to the other lands and henceforth the properties were owned separately.[4] This

---

(1) Lans. Mss. Vol. 88, fo. 189.
(2) Lans. Mss. Vol. 66, pp. 725-727.
(3) Lans. Mss. Vol. 88 f. 189.
(4) T. 77/9 Indenture of Feb. 21, 1781.

DR. ANDREW TURNBULL

was a great relief to Turnbull as he was now free, after being in custody for one year and seven months, but he vowed that as he was the victim of extortion, he would do all in his power to recover his property. He left Florida with his family and Mr. James Penman on May 7th, in a small sailing vessel which he chartered. Another small vessel with all that remained of his personal property was wrecked on the journey north, and so very much reduced in worldly possessions, he landed in Charleston May 13th. Tonyn's malignity never slumbered, however. He had even tried to persuade the captain not to take the Turnbulls and also wrote to Sir Henry Clinton at Charleston, saying he had heard that Mr. Penman was to act as Commissary and that Drayton and Turnbull expected to be employed in the army departments there. Therefore he had taken it upon himself to say that they were men of a desperate faction and ought not to hold office in the government.[1]

---

(1) Historical Mss. Commission, Amer. Mss. in Royal Institute, Vol. II, pp. 127-128.

THE NEW SMYRNA COLONY OF FLORIDA

As proof of Turnbull's alleged misconduct he declared that when the American army invaded Florida, Turnbull held aloof and did not offer to help make a stand. Turnbull heard of this charge and referred Germain to General Prevost to deny it, since he had traveled one hundred miles to the British camp on the St. John's to offer his services, which were accepted.[1] Thus by actual falsehood, as well as any other means in his power, Tonyn pursued his former Secretary. His influence did not reach Charleston, however, Lord Shelburne wrote to Cornwallis and Sir Guy Carleton in his behalf and Colonels Small and Moncrief and the powerful Drayton family easily convinced the authorities that Turnbull was being made a victim of personal enmity by Tonyn. So, just as Turnbull had vindicated Drayton in Florida, Drayton defended Turnbull in Charleston against their old enemy. The two men remained close friends

---

(1) C.O. 5/158, pp. 465-468.

DR. ANDREW TURNBULL

and Drayton's name appears as executor of Turnbull's will.[1]

Turnbull arrived in Charleston May 13, 1782, and on December 14th of the same year Charleston was evacuated by the British. Turnbull wrote to Shelburne that as Tonyn held the papers he must give the Auditors of the New Smyrna Estate, he felt obliged to stay there and try to get them, rather than return to England without them.[2] In a footnote to a list of claims, with remarks by Mr. Geo. Miller,[3] there is an interesting account of what happened to Turnbull under these conditions:

> "Immediately after the evacuation of Charleston Dr. Turnbull and Mr. James Penman were required to become citizens, which they refusing to do, and being men of respectable character, the matter was left to the decision of a committee of the Legislature then sitting, who agreed that they should remain as His Majesty's subjects; the only instance, I believe of the kind, that happened between the Evacuation of this Province and the peace, which redounds much to

---

(1) Probate Records, Charleston Co. S. C. Book B, p. 636.
(2) Lans. Mss. Vol. 88 f. 189.
(3) Treasury 77/20 (4).

their honour, since it is at once a proof of their sturdy Loyalty and the high respect in which their Characters were held."

Andrew Turnbull, Jr., also was included in the Certificates

"of their being His Majesty's subjects and in no sense Citizens of any of the United States * * * and have produced proof to me that they pay the Alien Duty (i.e. 4% ad valorem on goods imported into the province)."

And so Turnbull stuck to his determination of remaining a British subject in the face of all suspicion. He had said to Germain, "It is probable that Govr. Tonyn flatters himself of being able to drive me, thro' Despair, to such a Step, but he will find himself grossly mistaken, for the Amor Patriae, and of the British Constitution, while it lasts, will always hold me fast as a British Subject, which, however, is not meant to imply, that I am in love with the present Ministers, nor with their Measures,"[1] he concluded dryly.

---

(1) British Transcripts, Box 41, Lans. Mss. Vol. 1219, fo. 40.

DR. ANDREW TURNBULL

This loyalty was all the more praiseworthy when it is known that he was still in sore financial straits as a result of Germain's latest policy of simply letting the trouble with Tonyn wait until the greater question of the rebellious colonies was settled.

To relieve some of the burden of his father's large family, Nichol Turnbull had stayed at St. Augustine as Assistant to the Deputy Commissary of Provisions, and though he had a good education took the first work that offered itself, issuing rations to the garrison. The two oldest girls had married but their husbands died at the very beginning of their careers, and one young widow had returned to her father with her two children, while the other had remarried. Three sons still at school and the child of one of Turnbull's friends (who had been persecuted to his death by Tonyn, in the opinion of Turnbull) lived at home, making a family of nine people dependent upon the efforts of the doctor, now in his sixty-second year.

Van de Sande Studio, New Smyrna, Fla.

THE NEW SMYRNA COLONY OF FLORIDA

When Turnbull wrote again to Germain, he said he had left Florida and would never return while Tonyn was governor.[1] Germain therefore accepted his resignation and his former Deputy, Mr. Yeats, became Secretary. Mr. Yeats was the husband of Tonyn's niece and therefore very acceptable to the governor. The state of New Smyrna by 1783 may be judged from the following description attached to one of the grants:

> "I was at Smirna last in November 1783. The place was very well situated for trade being so near the Inlet; and the Country round it for planting as the land was of a good quality, the river also abounded in a remarkable degree with various kinds of fish—I had the curiosity when there to count all the houses both in Town and Country and to the best of my recollection there were some few more than one hundred fram'd buildings left standing, or unburnt, including those in the homble—Grenville's part—many of them were inhabited by Refugees at that time."[2]

Governor Tonyn's undisputed authority was short-lived, however. On September 3, 1783,

---

(1) C.O. 5/158, pp. 465-468.
(2) Treasury 77/7, Memo.—Schedule and Valuation of Lady Mary Duncan's estate.

DR. ANDREW TURNBULL

a treaty was promulgated whereby Florida was ceded to Spain and the English were given eighteen months to get out or become Catholics. The heaviness of this calamity to the English inhabitants must be described to be appreciated. For twenty years the English government had induced many wealthy men to aid in the settlement of Florida and in 1778 alone nearly seven thousand loyal planters had been persuaded to leave the rebel colonies,[1] so that they were now unable, on account of their open stand against America, to return to the United States. It may be imagined that Governor Tonyn was not popular with these men then. The property of the planters consisted mainly of lands and slaves, and when they were obliged to sell at once to any Spaniard willing or in any way able to buy, the result was ruinous. The British government sent a fleet of transports to Amelia Harbor at the mouth of the St.

---

(1) Fairbanks' History of Florida, (3d Ed.), p. 176.

Mary's river to take the refugees away, and there ensued as melancholy a spectacle as that of the Acadian deportation from Nova Scotia. Families and friends said goodbye forever and left their beautiful Florida homes, some for England, others for Nova Scotia, the Bahamas and Jamaica. The Minorcans gave Tonyn to understand that they intended to leave also, and some actually were sent to Dominica, the Bahamas and Europe.[1] But when Governor de Zespedes came to Florida in June, 1784, he brought a promotion for Pietro Campo, the Minorcan priest, and soon the majority of the Minorcans were firmly ensconsed as Spanish subjects. This seemed to be a distinct disappointment to Tonyn, who wrote Lord Sydney that he considered it a violation of the treaty of peace.[2]

Since old settlers who had moved from the colonies to Florida before the Revolution were

---

(1) C.O. 5/561, pp. 359-361.
(2) C.O. 5/561, pp. 359-361.

DR. ANDREW TURNBULL

able to return to the United States without the stigma of being refugee loyalists,[1] Turnbull felt himself lucky to be received cordially in Charleston, among this number. He soon made a wide reputation in his profession, becoming one of the first members of the South Carolina Medical Society.[2]

The settling of his affairs at New Smyrna continued to be a mournful burden to him, however. On May 2, 1786, hearing that Parliament had finally decided to reimburse former Florida landowners, he made Mr. James Penman, (then living in London as a merchant) attorney for himself and his children, to present their claims for indemnity for the loss of their lands in the cession of Florida.[3] In December of the same year his partners presented a memorial of their losses also, to which the names of former Florida witnesses were

---

(1) Fairbanks' Hist. of Florida, p. 240.
(2) Address of M. Michel before Med. Soc. South Carolina, Pamphlets Q No. 18, Charleston Library.
(3) T. 77/7.

attached. From this List we learn that Tonyn had been made a Major General for his services, and Grant a Lieutenant General,[1] so evidently the ministers were not displeased with the final disposition of affairs in Florida.

On March 14, 1788, Mr. Penman succeeded in getting a small part of Turnbull's claim. He had filed two, one for Turnbull himself, for real property, to the amount of £6462.10. for which he received nothing, the other for himself and children for £15057.10. for which he received £916.13.4.[2] Considering that some erstwhile Florida landowners died in want before help reached them, Turnbull was probably fortunate to have recovered the small amount he did. At any rate, it was a material recognition of his loyalty and good conduct as a British subject, after Tonyn's storms of abuse had subsided.

Both Turnbull and Drayton were active men

---

(1) T. 77/7.
(2) C.O. 5/562. Reports of Commissioners for Florida claims.

DR. ANDREW TURNBULL

of affairs up to the time of their deaths. Drayton was appointed Judge of the Admiralty Court of South Carolina in 1789, and died the following year. Turnbull died two years afterwards, March 13, 1792. His will[1] is a remarkable expression of his amiable and generous nature. He provided that his wife who was eleven years younger than himself, should remain as an executrix of his will whether she married again or not, and should inherit two-tenths of his estate without the power to give it away before her death, "because her good nature and love for her children might induce her to part with her share and be in distress." Gracia did not marry again, however. In a corner of the old portion of St. Philip's church yard at Charleston, now seldom unlocked, there is a small headstone, which reads:

>"Sacred to the
>Memory of
>Maria Gracia Turnbull, Relict
>and Consort of Dr. Andrew Turnbull.
>She departed this life Aug. 2nd,
>1798, aged 68 years."

---

(1) Probate Records, Charleston Co., S. C. Book B, p. 636.

THE NEW SMYRNA COLONY OF FLORIDA

No stone of any kind marks Turnbull's grave, but his obituary stated that he was to be buried there. This quaintly worded document, published in the Charleston Gazette, ends—"his name will long live and his virtues be held in the most pleasing remembrance, when this inconsiderable tribute of respect to his memory will be consigned to oblivion."[1] The tide of subsequent events made strange mock of this remark. For a time everyone forgot about Florida. Scattered in other lands— back in England, away in Nova Scotia or suffering from the jealous policy of their own people in Jamaica, the English exiles of Florida gave little thought to the bitter feuds which had seemed so engrossing to them for the last few years of English rule there. A force beyond their control had borne down upon them and swept them off forever from that strenuous, happy life, leaving them no connection with it thenceforth. Spain settled

---

(1) Charleston City Gazette, March 14, 1792.

DR. ANDREW TURNBULL

once more upon her scanty Florida nest, pursued her usual unenterprising course, and the splendid plantations, which had been built up with so much blood and toil, sank back into the forest, occasionally plundered by Indians, but more permanently injured by ignorance and neglect. Thirty-seven years afterwards, when Spain ceded Florida to the United States, of the English occupation there remained hardly a scratch upon the unkempt face of the wilderness, and the New Smyrna colony had become little more than a memory.

BIBLIOGRAPHY

ORIGINAL SOURCES

(Note: References such as C.O. 5/544 mean Colonial Office, Class 5, Vol. 544; P. C., Privy Council; W.O., War Office; A.O., Audit Office; T., Treasury.)

C.O. 5/548 pp. 363-366	18 June, 1766—Order in Council at Court of St. James of first land grant to Turnbull.
Pp. 365-367	18 June, 1766—Like order to Sir William Duncan.
Pp. 362-367	15 Jan., 1767—Minutes of Council of East Fla. Turnbull appointed to Council.
P. 368	17 Jan., 1767—Warrants of survey for Turnbull's and Duncan's lands.
P. 394	23 June, 1767—Warrant of survey for 1000 acres for Turnbull.
Privy Council Register, Vol. 112	13 May, 1767—Orders in Council.
C.O. 5/541 p. 215	April, 1767—Turnbull's petition for the East Florida bounty.

197

DR. ANDREW TURNBULL

C.O. 5/541 p. 272	Return of grants of land in East Florida between 20 June, 1765 and 22 June, 1767.
C.O. 5/544 pp. 37-42	29 Aug., 1767—Gov. Grant to Hillsborough, Turnbull's arrival in Florida.
British Transcripts, Box 252, Library of Congress, Washington, D. C.	Mar. 31, 1767—Shelburne to the Lords of Trade on advisability of Turnbull's colony.
C.O. 5/563 pp. 226-228	Apr. 16, 1767—Endorsement and grant of bounty by Lords of Trade for Turnbull's colony.
Privy Council, Register, Vol. 112	May 13, 1767—Grant of 5000 acres to each of Turnbull's four children.
	May 13, 1767—Order in Council appointing Turnbull to East Florida council.
C.O. 5/548	May 14, 1767—Shelburne to Governor of Florida, granting bounty to Turnbull.
C.O. 5/549 p. 49	Dec. 25, 1767—Grant to Hillsborough. He had four months' provisions awaiting settlers at New Smyrna.
C.O. 5/549 p. 54	Feb. 23, 1768—Hillsborough to Grant. Thinks Turnbull's plan the best idea so far for development of Florida.
Kings Mss. 211, British Museum	1768 Vol. II—Survey ad brief comment on New Smyrna by Wm. Gerard de Brahm.
C.O. 5/549 p. 75	Mar. 10, 1768—Hillsborough to Grant. Turnbull sailing from Minorca.

THE NEW SMYRNA COLONY OF FLORIDA

C.O. 5/549 pp. 77-78	Mar. 12, 1768—Grant to Hillsborough. Turnbull at Milo on Sept. 24, and now expected daily.
C.O. 5/549 p. 81	May 12, 1768—Hillsborough to Grant. Turnbull at Gibraltar with 1000 colonists.
C.O. 5/541 pp. 423-424	July 2, 1768—Grant to Hillsborough, Turnbull's Colony the largest which ever came to America in one body.
C.O. 5/541 p. 427	July 2, 1768—Names of the eight ships and number of colonists in each, 1403 people in all.
C.O. 5/544 pp. 37-42	Aug. 29, 1768—Grant to Hillsborough. The mutiny at New Smyrna.
C.O. 5/549 p. 262	Sept. 14, 1768—Hillsborough to Grant. The King wishes Turnbull success.
C.O. 5/544 pp. 95-96	Oct. 20, 1768—Grant to Hillsborough. The leaders of the munity captured.
C.O. 5/544 pp. 99-102	Dec. 1, 1768—Grant to Hillsborough. Great size of colony makes government aid necessary.
C.O. 5/549 p. 339	Dec. 10, 1768—Hillsborough to Grant. The King concerned to hear of munity and approves Grant's action in lending aid to Turnbull.
C.O. 5/544 p. 187	Jan. 3, 1769—Grant to Hillsborough. Thinks government aid would be needed for such extensive plan.
C.O. 5/544 pp. 192-193	Jan. 14, 1769—Grant to Hillsborough. Order restored at New Smyrna after two ringleaders in munity executed.

DR. ANDREW TURNBULL

C.O. 5/544 pp. 200-201	Mar. 4, 1769—Grant to Hillsborough. Seven miles cleared but money needed at New Smyrna.
C.O. 5/550 p. 67	Mar. 30, 1769—2000 pounds from British Board of Trade and Plantations for relief of New Smyrna.
C.O. 5/550 pp. 72-73	April 3, 1769—Hillsborough to Grant. Approval of execution of two and pardon of rest of mutineers at New Smyrna.
C.O. 5/550 p. 97	June 7, 1769—Hillsborough to Grant. The King approves of Grant's policy at New Smyrna, but warns him not to spend beyond Parliamentary grant.
C.O. 5/544 p. 205	July 20, 1769—Grant to Hillsborough. Vines planted and Barilla tried by Turnbull. Indigo, cotton and rice shipped.
C.O. 5/544 pp. 213-214	July 21, 1769—Grant to Hillsborough. Colony has cost proprietors 28,000 pounds. Too large for private undertaking.
C.O. 5/544 pp. 221-222	Sept. 18, 1769—Grant to Hillsborough. Relief shall not exceed amount granted New Smyrna.
C.O. 5/550 pp. 137-138	Nov. 4, 1769—Hillsborough to Grant. Approval of Grant's pardon of three mutineers.
C.O. 5/545 pp. 33-34	Sept. 1, 1770—Grant to Hillsborough. Turnbull needs 1000 pounds for clothes and equipment. Indent included of articles needed.

THE NEW SMYRNA COLONY OF FLORIDA

C.O. 5/545 p 45	Oct. 2, 1770—Grant to Hillsborough. Mr. De Brahm refused to allow letters to be carried on his vessel, causing Grant some trouble with supplies at New Smyrna.
C.O. 5/551 pp. 157-158	Dec. 11, 1770—Hillsborough to Grant. Government cannot grant any further bounty to New Smyrna.
C.O. 5/545 p. 74	Dec. 14, 1770—Grant to Hillsborough. Road needed to plantations of Turnbull and others at Mosquitoes.
C.O. 5/552 p. 38	February 15, 1771—Grant to Hillsborough. Last of bounty accounted for at New Smyrna.
C.O. 5/552 p. 25	Mar. 8, 1771—Robinson to Pownall. Lords of Trade cannot grant further bounty to New Smyrna.
C.O. 5/545 p. 81-82	Mar. 20, 1771—Grant to Hillsborough. Bounty will not be granted unless Hillsborough urges measure before Lords of Trade.
C.O. 5/545 p. 85	Mar. 20, 1771—Grant to Hillsborough. Turnbull could not be governor on account of his colony and will not interfere with Moultrie's appointment.
C.O. 5/552 p. 30	April 1, 1771—Hillsborough to Grant. Regrets inability of government to grant further bounty at New Smyrna.
C.O. 5/552 pp. 97-99	May 9, 1771—Turnbull to Grant or Moultrie. Indians frighten settlers at Mosquitoes.

DR. ANDREW TURNBULL

C.O. 5/552 pp. 85-88-89	May 23, 1771—Moultrie to Hillsborough. No cause for anxiety over Indians at New Smyrna.
C.O. 5/552 pp. 101-102	June 6, 1771—Moultrie to McKenzie. Asks for detachment of troops to guard New Smyrna from Indians.
C.O. 5/552 p. 105	June 6, 1771—McKenzie to Moultrie. Refuses troops.
C.O. 5/552 pp. 91-94	June 13, 1771—Moultrie to Hillsborough. Complains of Turnbull's varying reports and McKenzie's refusal.
C.O. 5/546 pp. 100-101	Sept. 25, 1771—Moultrie to Hillsborough. Fine road completed to New Smyrna.
C.O. 5/545 p. 123-124	Oct. 20, 1771—Moultrie to Hillsborough. Turnbull's constant residence at his colony makes him rare attendant in Council.
C.O. 5/552 p. 123	Dec. 4, 1771—Hillsborough to Moultrie. Glad alarm over Indians at Mosquitoes has subsided.
C.O. 5/546 p. 136	Dec. 28, 1771—Moultrie to Hillsborough. Drayton and Turnbull resign from Council.
C.O. 5/545 pp. 206-207	Aug. 20, 1772—Moultrie to Hillsborough. Mr. Forbes made visiting Minister to Mosquitoes.
C.O. 5/545 pp. 289-290	Feb. 19, 1773—Moultrie to Dartmouth. Prosperity and good humor at New Smyrna.

THE NEW SMYRNA COLONY OF FLORIDA

C.O. 5/555 p. 281	Nov. 23, 1774—Copy of Bryan's letter to Drayton on Indian lands dispute.
C.O. 5/555 pp. 53-60	Dec. 30, 1774—Tonyn to Dartmouth. Condemns Drayton for part in Indian lands quarrel.
C.O. 5/555 pp. 227-281	Drayton's complete account of Indian lands question presented to Tonyn.
C.O. 5/556 pp. 117-118	Nov. 1, 1775—Tonyn to Dartmouth. Further complaints of Drayton, Turnbull and Penman for trying to run the province.
C.O. 5/556 p. 55	Dec. 20, 1775—Address of praise by Grand Jury headed by Turnbull and directed to Drayton.
C.O. 5/556 pp. 501-502	Feb. 15, 1776—Governor threatens Turnbull if he sides with Drayton.
C.O. 5/556 pp. 113-115	Feb. 27, 1776—Address of loyalty to King headed by Turnbull.
C.O. 5/556 p. 463	Mar. 4, 1776—Tonyn to Turnbull. Demands explanation for public defense of Drayton.
C.O. 5/556 p. 105	Mar. 7, 1776—Turnbull to Tonyn. Two hundred men at New Smyrna of military age.
C.O. 5/556 pp. 89-93	Mar. 15, 1776—Turnbull to Tonyn. Sarcastic reply to Tonyn's reprimand for siding with Drayton.
C.O. 5/556 pp. 97-100	Mar. 18, 1776—Tonyn to Turnbull. Intends to charge him before Council.

DR. ANDREW TURNBULL

C.O. 5/556 pp. 73-77	Mar. 22, 1776—Tonyn to Germain. An opposition loyal address and complaints of Drayton's faction.
C.O. 5/556 pp. 505-512	Mar. 30, 1776—Minutes of East Florida Council suspending Turnbull, with minority opposition.
C.O. 5/556 pp. 495-498	Apr. 2, 1776—Tonyn to Germain. Accuses Turnbull and Drayton of disloyalty.
C.O. 5/556 p. 109	May 10, 1776—Turnbull to Germain. Presents address and asks audience.
C.O. 5/556 pp. 232-235	June 14, 1776—Germain to Tonyn. Reprimand, and full reinstatement of Drayton.
C.O. 5/556 p. 245	July 1, 1776—Turnbull to Germain. Asks for extension of leave of absence.
C.O. 5/568 pp. 337-338	July 19, 1776—Tonyn to Germain. Indian disorders at New Smyrna.
C.O. 5/556 p. 744	Aug. 21, 1776—Tonyn to Germain. Can raise only one Company at New Smyrna.
C.O. 5/556 p. 767	Sept. 1, 1776—Turnbull, Jr., to Gordon. Unrest at Mosquitoes caused by American invasion.
C.O. 5/556 pp. 771-772	Sept. 10, 1776—Bisset to Tonyn. Fears disloyalty among Minorcans.
C.O. 5/556 p. 765	Sept. 8, 1776—Tonyn to Germain. Has always doubted New Smyrna's advantages to province, and now finds it in state of unrest.

THE NEW SMYRNA COLONY OF FLORIDA

Lans. Vol. 1919 fo. 40	Mar. 16, 1780—Turnbull to Germain. Full arraignment of Tonyn and of Germain himself for tolerating him.
Historical Mss. Commission Amer. Mss. in Royal Institution Vol. II, pp. 127-128	May 27, 1780—Tonyn to Clinton. Tries to prejudice him against Drayton, Turnbull and Penman.
C.O. 5/158 pp. 465-468	June 15, 1781—Turnbull to Germain. Will never return to Florida until Tonyn removed from office.
Treasury 77/20(4)	May, 1780—Turnbull and Penman allowed to remain in Charleston as British subjects.
C.O. 5/560 pp. 289-290	July 25, 1781—Tonyn to Germain. Evacuation of Florida progressing well except for Minorcans.
T. 77/9	Mar. 9 and Oct. 2, 1781—Various agreements between Turnbull and partners during life of the colony.
T. 77/7	Nov., 1783—Refugees hiding in many of the 100 unburnt buildings at New Smyrna.
T. 77/7	May 6, 1784—Schedule and valuation of Grenville, Duncan and Turnbull lands in Florida.
C.O. 5/561 pp. 359-361	Apr. 4, 1785—Tonyn to Germain. Will be no more than 3 or 4 British left in Florida.
T. 77/17	May 2, 1786—Turnbull gives Penman power of attorney to try to obtain reimbursement from government

DR. ANDREW TURNBULL

	for loss of land in cession of Florida.
T. 77/7	Dec. 30, 1786—Grenville and Duncan heirs file claim for similar reimbursements with full account of the business transactions of the colony.
C.O. 5/546 pp. 49-51	Sept. 19, 1776—Turnbull before Lords of Trade, with charges against Tonyn.
C.O. 5/556 pp. 695-697	Nov. 6, 1776—Germain to Tonyn. Reproof for treatment of Turnbull.
C.O. 5/546 pp. 53-54	Dec. 6, 1776—Another list of charges against Tonyn by Turnbull.
C.O. 391/83 p. 20	Dec. 10, 1776—Lords of Trade demand explanation from Tonyn.
C.O. 5/155	Jan. 30, 1778—Turnbull to Germain. Asks reinstatement in office.
C.O. 324/43 p. 413	July 11, 1776—King grants extended leave of absence from Florida to Turnbull.
C.O. 5/546 pp. 77-85	Feb. 17, 1777—Defense of Turnbull to charges made by Tonyn. (No charges regarding Minorcans).
C.O. 5/546 p. 75	Feb. 17, 1777—Turnbull asks Lords of Trade to reinstate him in office.
C.O. 5/557 pp. 115-121	Apr. 14, 1777—Germain to Tonyn. Reinstatement of Turnbull and reproof for Tonyn.
C.O. 5/557 pp. 225-226	May 8, 1777—Yonge to Tonyn. Minorcans file complaints against Turnbull.

THE NEW SMYRNA COLONY OF FLORIDA

C.O. 5/557 pp. 479-480	May 8, 1777—Affidavits of Minorcans.
Treasury 77/7	List of buildings completed by 1777 at New Smyrna and their cost.
C.O. 5/557 p. 420	May 8, 1777—Tonyn to Germain. Paying particular attention to New Smyrna.
Historical Mss. Commission Sackville Mss. Vol. II, p. 82	Dec. 8, 1777—Turnbull to Germain. Tonyn's illegal dealings ruining the settlement.
C.O. 5/558 pp. 101-103-104	Dec. 29, 1777—Tonyn to Germain. Tries to prove New Smyrna could never have been profitable.
C.O. 5/546 pp. 227-228	Jan. 19, 1778—Tonyn to Germain. An inaccurate resume of his quarrel with Drayton and Turnbull.
C.O. 5/558 p. 8	Feb. 19, 1778—Germain to Tonyn. Condemns the encouragement of desertion of New Smyrna by settlers.
C.O. 5/558 p. 495	May 4, 1778—Purcell to Tonyn. Complains that Turnbull accused him of falsehood.
C.O. 5/558 pp. 499-500	May 27, 1778—Tonyn to Purcell. Pompous defense of Purcell.
C.O. 5/558 p. 487	Aug. 7, 1778—Turnbull to Tonyn. Intends to live in St. Augustine and act as Secretary.
British Tran-	Aug. 11, 1778—Tonyn to Turnbull.

DR. ANDREW TURNBULL

scripts, Box 252 Library of Congress C.O. 5/158 p. 469	Refuses to allow him to act as Secretary.
Sackville Mss. America, 1755-7 No. 100	Dec. 8, 1777—Turnbull to Germain. A full account of Tonyn's persecution of him and bribery among Minorcans.
C.O. 5/569 p. 79	Aug. 20, 1778—Tonyn to Germain. 30 negroes carried off from New Smyrna.
C.O. 5/559 pp. 40-42	Aug. 27, 1778—Tonyn to Prevost. Desires troops to guard Mosquitoes.
C.O. 5/558 pp. 484-6	Sept. 26, 1778—Tonyn to Knox. "Will be inexpressible satisfaction to be of service to the unfortunate partners of Turnbull."
Br. Transcripts, Box 41, folio 47, Vol. 1219, Lansdowne Mss.	Feb. 17, 1780—Order placing Turnbull under arrest.
Lans. Mss. Vol. 1219, folio 49	Feb. 17, 1780—Demurrer of Turnbull to charges made against him.
Library of Congress, Br. Transcripts, Box 41, Lans. Mss. 1219, fo. 34	Mar. 14, 1780—Turnbull to Shelburne. Asks letter of introduction to Cornwallis and tells of his hopelessness over the situation.
Audit Office Declared Accts. Buncle 1261 Roll 154	Mar. 9, 1787—Account by Grant of 2000 pounds bounty spent at New Smyrna, 1769-70.

THE NEW SMYRNA COLONY OF FLORIDA

C.O. 5/562	Mar. 14, 1788—Report of Commissioners for East Florida claims. Turnbull received £916. 13. 4.
City Gazette and Daily Advertiser, Charleston, S. C.	Mar. 14, 1792—Obituary of Turnbull.
Probate Records, Charleston, Co., S. C. Book B. p. 636	Mar. 17, 1792—Will of Turnbull.
S. C. Pamphlets 2, No. 18 Charleston Library	Address of M. Michel before Medical Society. Turnbull one of first members of Society.

LANSDOWNE MSS.

Vol. 88, f. 133	Sept. 1, 1766—A. Turnbull to E. of Shelburne, enclosing Dr. Turnbull's Narrative.
Vol. 52, pp. 294-288-289	Jan. 17 and 29, 1767—A. Turnbull to E. of Shelburne (abst.) with abstract of reply, May 14, 1767.
Vol. 52, f. 139	May 1, 1767—A. Turnbull to E. of Shelburne (abst.)
Vol. 52, f. 135	July 10, 1767—A. Turnbull to E. of Shelburne.
Vol. 52, f. 147	Feb. 27, 1768—A. Turnbull to E. of Shelburne. (Ext. and Abst.)
Vol. 52, f. 151	Mar. 28, 1768—A. Turnbull to E. of Shelburne. (Ext.)
Vol. 52, f. 145	Apr. 4, 1768—A. Turnbull to E. of Shelburne.
Vol. 52, f. 155	Sept. 24, 1769—A. Turnbull to E. of Shelburne. (Ext.)

DR. ANDREW TURNBULL

Vol. 52, f. 157	Oct. 3, 1774—A. Turnbull to E. of Shelburne. (Ext.)
Vol. 52, f. 163	Nov. 10, 1777—A. Turnbull to E. of Shelburne. (Ext.)
Vol. 52, f. 173	Dec. 16, 1777—A. Turnbull to E. of Shelburne.
Vol. 52, f. 175	Dec. 23, 1777—A. Turnbull to E. of Shelburne. (Ext.)

SECONDARY SOURCES

Avarette, Mrs. A.
    The Unwritten History of St. Augustine.

Bartram, Wm.
    Travels Through North and South Carolina, Georgia and East and West Florida.
        London, 1794.

Brinton, D. G.
    Notes on the Floridian Peninsula.
        Philadelphia, 1859.
    Florida and the South.

Dewhurst, Wm. W.
    History of Saint Augustine, Florida.
        New York, 1885

Fairbanks, George R.
    History of Florida.
        1871.
    History and Antiquities of St. Augustine, Florida.
        New York, 1858.
    Spaniards of Florida.

Forbes
    Sketches, Historical and Topographical of the Floridas.
        New York, 1821.

Lanier, Sidney
    Florida, Its Scenery, Climate and History.
        Philadelphia, 1875.

DR. ANDREW TURNBULL

Lecky, Wm. Edward
 A History of England in the Eighteenth Century, Vol. III.
 New York, 1891.

Mease, James M.
 Bulletin B de la Societe De Geographie, V. VII.
 Paris, 1827.

Romans, Capt. Bernard
 A Concise History of East and West Florida.
 New York, 1876.

Schoepf, Johann David
 Travels in the Confederation.
 (Trans. from German by A. J. Morrison).
 Philadelphia, 1911.

Sewell, R. K.
 Sketches of St. Augustine.
 New York, 1848.

Stoddard, Major Amos.
 Sketches, Historical and Descriptive, of Louisiana.
 Philadelphia, 1812.

Vignoles, Charles
 Observations upon the Floridas.
 New York, 1823.

Williams, J. L.
 Territory of Florida.
 New York, 1837.

INDEX

A

Address, of loyalty, 117; names, 118.
American Revolution, in Fla., 42, 89, 142.
Amelia Narrows, Americans at, 176.
Alortz, Fla., grantee, 86.

B

Bartram, Wm., author of Fla. Travels, 15, 23, 25, 75.
Barrington, Fla., grantee, 86.
Bella Vista, Moultrie's plantation, 87.
Bisset, Colonel, grantee, 86, 119, 141, 143.
Boston Massacre, 82, 119, 141, 143; Tea Party, 109; Port Bill, 109.
Brahm, Wm. Gerard de, surveyor general, 24.
Bryant, Langley, overseer, 102.
Bryant, Jonathan, Indian lands, 111-2.
Burdett, Sir Charles, Fla., grantee, 23.

C

Campbell, Fla., grantee, 86.
Campos, Don, Minorcan priest, 97-99.
Canals at New Smyrna, 93-4.
Carolinas, pioneer life, 46.
Carysfort, convoys Turnbull, 40.

Charleston, 14, 69, 180, 184; evacuation, 186; Gazette, 195.
Clinton, Sir Henry, 184.
Clark, Fla., grantee, 86.
Clotha Corona, Greek colonist, 52.
Colonists, characteristics of, 36.
Contracts with settlers, 31, 147, 163.
Coquina, Fla., rock, 49-50.
Cowsfort, early Jacksonville, 86.
Cowkeeper, Indian chief, 101; Council, in Fla., 102, 132.
Congress, First Continental, 109.
Creeks, Indian tribe in Ga., 14.
Cutter, English overseer, 52-56; death, 60.
Cumberland, his ignorance of American opinions, 41.

D

Daytona, contrast between modern and ancient, 51.
Drayton, Chief Justice, 23, 87, 88; quarrel with Moultrie, 90; Indian lands, 110-12; suspended, 115; at New Smyrna, 129; in England, 132; reinstatement, 139; on Minorcans, 169; in Charleston, 180, 185, 194.
Duncan, Sir William, partner of Turnbull, 18, 27, 73.

E

East Florida boundaries, 13; ship, 57.
Egmont, Fla., grantee, 86.
England, colonization policy, 14-15, 106; Express rider bearing urgent news, 54, 55.

F

Faucet, Fla., grantee, 86.
Florida, Spanish colony, 11; boundaries, 13; English colony, 89, 98, 105, 107, 109; receded to Spain, 190; American purchase, 196; climate, 15, 20-22.
Forbes, author of a Florida history, 90.
Forni, Carlo, Italian leader of uprising, 52.
Fort George, at St. Augustine, 87.
Forbes, Rev. John, Minister at St. Augustine, 85; admiralty judge, 23.
Frazier, Minister at New Smyrna, 23, 85.
Fuser, Lieut.-Col. 174, 176.

G

Gaspin, British ship destroyed, 105.
Georgia, colonial methods, 46; in Revolution, 109.
Germain, Lord George, 115, 134; on Drayton, 138-139; on Turnbull, 154-156, on New Smyrna, 169.
Gibraltar, Turnbull stops at, 38.
Gracia Dura Bin, wife of Turnbull, 16-18; at New Smyrna, 85; Tonyn's hostility, 172-173; her children, 182, 188; death, 194.
Graham, John, Ga. resident, 148.

Grayhurst, Fla., grantee, 86.
Grant, English Governor of Fla., 20; policy, 88; opinion of colonists, 37; opinion of Turnbull, 65-66, 78, 80; leaves Florida, 78; in England, 193.
Greece, settlers from, 29.
Grenville, colonial policy, 27; Turnbull's partner, 27; Indian lands, 73.

H

Havana, captured by English, 12; correspondence, 99.
Hauks, Fla., grantee, 86.
Hillsborough, e n c o u r a g e s large colony, 36; urges Turnbull for governor, 78-80; refuses further support to New Smyrna, 83.

I

Indent, list of articles for New Smyrna, 72.
Indians, allied to Spain, 11; Fla. tribes, 13-14; attitude towards New Smyrna, 37-38; 101, 140-141.

J

Jollie, Fla., councilman, on Turnbull, 133-134.

K

Keys, Florida, islands off Florida coast, 59.

L

Law, English, severe in Colonial days, 59-60.

M

MacKenzie, Major, commander east Fla. troops, 103.

Magnolia gardens, Drayton's home in Charleston, 180.
Marchmont, Lord, Tonyn's sponsor, 145.
Matanzas, inlet, 158.
Mann, 174.
Minorca, island, 32; religion, 32, 98; famine, 34.
Mobile, in British West Fla., 13.
Modon, Turnbull touches at, 30.
Mosquitoes, region near New Smyrna, 37; Inlet, 24, 25 26.
Moultrie, James, Lieut.-Gov. of Fla., 23, 80, 87, 100-105; on New Smyrna, 91; on Turnbull, 102; on Tonyn, 110.

N

New Smyrna, name, description, 25-27; partnership, 18-19, 73, 175; division of lands, 183; land grants, 19, 27; indemnity, 192-193; terms of grants, 32, 35, 147-148; provisions at 45, 69; gov. relief, 70; equipment, 166-167; summary of difficulties, 162-163; ruin, 189.
North, Lord, 136.

O

Oglethorpe, expedition against Fla., 12.
Ormond, contrast between modern and ancient, 51.
Oswald, Mt., plantation, 23, 51.

P

Peace of Paris, 12.
Peloponnesus, tribesmen of, 30.
Pensacola, in British West Florida, 13.
Penman, friend of Turnbull, 132, 148, 174, 184; in England, 192, 193.
Pitt, ignorance of American opinion, 41.
Pirates, on Fla. coast, 95; Barbary, Algerian, 40.
Planters, names of English, 23, 118; fate after Revolution, 190-191, 195.
Plymouth, pioneer life, 46.
Potts, Fla., grantee, 86.
Prevost, General, 174, 177.
Products at New Smyrna, 76.
Purcell, Joseph, Minorcan, 157, 167.

R

Roads, called King's roads, 86.
Rockingham, Cabinet hears views of Pitt, 42.
Rolls, Denis, Fla., grantee, 86.
Romans, Bernard, author of a Florida history, 15, 61, 158.

S

Sanche, Lewis, Minorcan, 160-161.
Sandy, Black, slave, 102.
Savannah, 69.
Scurvy, at New Smyrna, 63.
Schoepf, Johann, traveler in Fla., 75.
Ships, names of Turnbull's, 28; cargo, 39; voyage, 43.
Shelburne, Lord, sponsors New Smyrna, 28; out of favor, 82.
Slaves, escape to Fla., 11; for New Smyrna, 44; in Fla., 95.
Spain, colonizing policy, 13; plots in Fla., 97, 99.
Stamp Act, effect on colonization, 41.

Stark, Wm., Fla., grantee, 23.
Strachey, Fla., grantee, 86.
St. Augustine, 13; English, at, 20; houses, 21, 44; society, 87; dissention, 176.
St. John's Bluff, on river, 177.
St. Mary's river, northern border of Fla., 86.

T

Taylor, Fla., grantee, 86.
Temple, Lord, partner of Turnbull, 18, 27, 73.
Tonyn, Gov. of Fla., 106; proclamations, 106, 109; quarrel with Drayton, 113; with Turnbull, 120, 132, 153, 180, 184-185; in England, 193; on American Revolution, 174.
Turnbull, Doctor Andrew, previous life, 16; in Fla., 19; position, 24, 77; Grant on, 65-66; election dispute, 90; Indian lands, 110, 116; on Tonyn, 145-152; in Charleston, 186, 188, 192; death, 194; obituary, 195.

Turnbull, Andrew, nephew of Doctor, 85, 142-143, 187.
Turnbull, Nichol, son of Doctor, 188.

U

Uprising of 1768, 52-60; Minorcans' attitude, 53-55; Greeks and Italians in, 53; losses, 60; summary, 61-62.

V

Visitors to colony, 49, 85.

W

West Florida boundaries, 12.
Waldron, Fla., grantee, 86.
Warron, Fla., grantee, 86.
Wright, Fla., grantee, 86.

Y

Yeats, Fla., secretary after Turnbull, 189.
Yemassee Indians, hostile to Creek tribes and Spaniards, 101.

www.ingramcontent.com/pod-product-compliance
Lightning Source LLC
Chambersburg PA
CBHW051048160426
43193CB00010B/1104